The Machine Embroiderer's Workbook

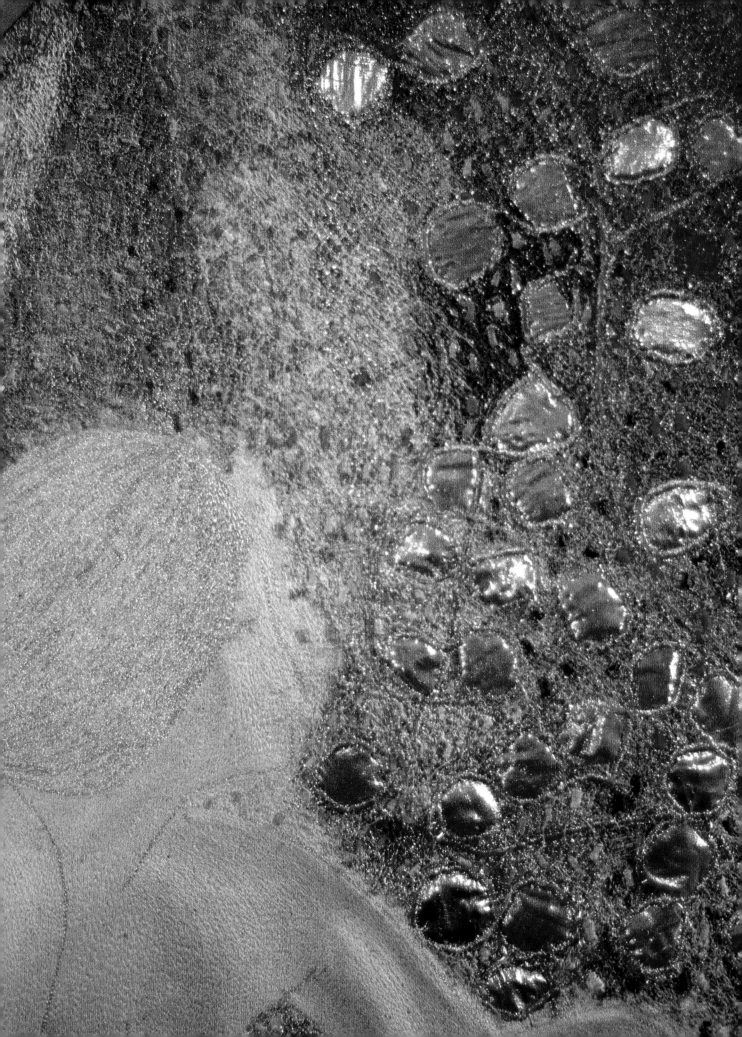

The Machine Embroiderer's Workbook

Val Holmes

B T Batsford Ltd London

ISBN 0 7134 7983 3

Photoset by Deltatype Ltd, Ellesmere Port, Cheshire
and printed in Hong Kong

for the publishers
B.T. Batsford Ltd
4 Fitzhardinge Street
London W1H 0AH

Page 1

Danae being seduced by Zeus *Hanging 132cm (52in) square,
worked completely on silk. The theme of the seduction of Danae by Zeus,
who descends in a shower of gold, has been well used by artists through the
centuries and much has been written about contemporary views of women
as portrayed in Danae. My Danae accepts the status and the wealth of her
suitor, but is bored by it.*

*The hanging is worked in appliqué and patchwork; some of the fabrics
are dyed and painted with metallic dyes. The four central panels are closed
and tied with ribbon.*

Page 2

*A close up of the embroidery. Scrim is stitched and pulled with metallic
zigzag stitching, this is then applied to a ground of silk noile with gold nets
and tissues. Further stitching is added. Danae is worked directly onto the
silk noile with straight stitching.*

Page 3

Danae being seduced by Zeus *The hanging opened. The four
central triangular sections fold back and are tied with ribbons to reveal the
action. Thus the viewer takes part in the action and can choose to become a
voyeur.*

Contents

Acknowledgements

Almost all of the drawings and samples were prepared specifically to illustrate this book. All work is mine unless otherwise acknowledged.

Thank you to Richard Bird for photographing all the work, with the exception of numbers 2, 56 and 82, which were photographed by myself, and 3, 76 and 77 which were photographed by Bob Garnet.

Many thanks to Martin Holmes and Roma and Peter Edge for their constant support, and of course, proof reading. Thank you to all the embroiderers who contributed work, and to the many others whose work was not included because of pressure of space in a small book which attempts to cover so many techniques. Thank you too to the owners of some of my pieces who allowed me to borrow them for photography.

I would also like to thank Bernina and Pfaff for being so helpful in providing a machine (the latter) and machine tools (the former) and illustrations. For most of the embroideries it is irrelevant which make of machine was used, but occasionally I have acknowledged a machine to give an idea as to the scope of work that can be done. Thanks also to Madeira Threads UK Ltd and the Campden Needlecraft Centre, Chipping Campden, for extensive help with materials.

V.H. 1991

Introduction

Machine embroidery is a technique that both intimidates and fascinates many embroiderers. In this book I have aimed to provide clear instruction to introduce the uninitiated so that confidence and skills can be acquired and built on. I hope that the instructions will also help those with some experience to understand and more thoroughly master their machines. The book is presented as a course, and it is intended that students may actually work through from chapter 1 to the end – thus a thorough portfolio of skills will be accumulated. However, it is possible to dip into a chapter here and there in order to learn a specific skill or try a new idea. Experienced machine embroiderers will find the first three chapters of interest mostly as a refresher course, but hopefully the further chapters will offer interesting ideas and new skills to many.

It has taken the mainstream of embroidery practice nearly a century to accept machine embroidery as valid in the field of craft or 'fine art' embroidery. To many it represented a process that had industrial rather than hand worked or individually produced craft connotations. To others a machine was thought to be 'cheating'; as a method of emulating hand embroidery it was thought inadequate, and it perhaps needed the artistic skills of people such as Rebecca Crompton to show that machine embroidery had a style of its own and could be seen as a legitimate craft in its own right. Nevertheless there are still diehards who insist that machine embroidery is somehow cheating, and it is through producing well-designed, carefully thought out and competently executed machine embroidery that we will finally be able to convince even the most doubting.

There are essential differences between the qualities of hand and machine embroidery, although by using various techniques the two methods can overlap, and in some instances successfully emulate each other. Understanding the differences in the qualities produced is essential if these qualities are to be exploited to the best advantage in embroideries.

Machine stitching essentially produces an unbroken line, whereas hand stitchery can more easily create broken and disassociated marks. Obviously there are methods by which machine embroidery can create what appears to be unrelated marks, and many hand stitches exist which create unbroken lines; but it is these characteristics that most especially identify the strengths of the two methods. The unbroken machine line can be produced quickly and with a freshness in its drawing that is often lacking in hand work, thus offering a useful area to exploit. The unbroken

line can also be used like a crayoning mark, colour can be built up by laying lines of thread side by side, and additional colours can be overlaid in a similar manner to crayon and pastel drawings. Drawing fine lines or building up areas or layers of colour can become quite laborious if attempted by hand, and so these methods of design are ideal in machine stitchery. Because an interlocked unbroken line is made with a sewing machine, it also makes this an ideal method of stitching on vanishing fabrics thus creating a type of lacy texture that is impossible by hand.

There are also less easily created or obvious areas of machine embroidery where a similar effect to some hand work can be achieved, replacing a process that can be tediously repetitive or time consuming.

Threads and ribbons can be couched and added by machine in a variety of ways, some of which look very similar to simple hand couching. Thicker threads can be added and surfaces built up using various methods, creating texture in a technique that many regard as only suitable for creating painterly and low key surfaces.

Machine embroidery can also be used to good effect to create openwork embroidery – pulled work, eyelets, insertion stitches and cutwork. Of course, using hand stitch ideas need only be a starting point for creating original designs using unusual techniques in machine embroidery.

To achieve machine embroidery of a high standard a great deal of care must be taken. Designing and sampling must be thorough, as with any embroidery. It is important to choose the right type of stitch for an area, or method of laying down straight stitches to create the desired texture. Attention must be paid to the stitching whilst working. Remember that when working by hand each stitch is carefully considered and placed, and its colour and the texture of the yarn are also thought out. Machine embroidery must be done with as much care if the work is to look good and not be untidy, but your thinking about placement and texture of stitches will have to be done at a greater speed; the needle position and where it enters the fabric must be watched constantly and carefully.

The right materials

The choice of threads, fabrics and needles is also important. If the design is to include a lot of machine embroidery it is very likely that the work will end up out of shape and perhaps lumpy. So with heavily worked embroidery it is important that a natural fabric is used as these more readily respond than synthetics to stretching back into shape. Stretching machine embroidery is covered in the Conclusion to this book.

There are a number of reasons why it is better to choose machine embroidery threads, rather than just ordinary sewing cottons:

- Machine embroidery threads are specifically made for the purpose and are smoother and usually finer.
- A wider colour range is available, including shaded threads and multicolours as well as various qualities of metallic threads.
- Because greater quantities are included on a reel they work out considerably cheaper.
- Machine embroidery threads, being softer, can produce finer lines and subtler colour build-up and shading – sewing threads tend to produce thicker, scratchier lines.
- Having a looser twist than ordinary threads, they are softer and spread more easily to cover areas or create satin stitch.
- A variety of thicknesses are available which should suit different purposes, from thick quilted lines to fine painterly areas of colour. Each embroiderer will have a favourite thickness which suits their style of work. I prefer 40s and 50s thickness, finding these suitable and versatile for anything I wish to achieve.

The choice of needles is also important – a wide variety of sizes is available in both sharp and ballpoint. As a general rule it is best to choose the finest available (70s or 80s) so that large holes are not made in the fabric when stitching. Certain threads may require a larger needle (90 or 100) in order to run through smoothly without fear of breaking; or if the work is particularly hard, through a build-up of fabrics or threads, a larger needle is useful. Ballpoint needles are specifically designed for use with synthetic fabric as they push the fibres apart, making a hole for entry rather than trying to break through these harder fibres. They can be particularly useful for fine silk, quilting and vanishing fabrics.

The right machine

Choosing a sewing machine is also an important step, particularly because of the costs involved. The following features should be considered when deciding if an existing machine is suitable for machine embroidery or when purchasing a new machine:

- It must be electrically operated (leaving both hands free to work) and provide an even, controllable speed.
- The machine motion should stop as soon as the foot pressure is removed and not run on. Ideally the machine will also have a choice of speeds (two is usual). The latest machines are controllable to the extent that one single stitch is possible, and often a modern electronic machine will have a button where the final needle position can be selected as up or down – a luxury perhaps, but very useful and something to be considered if making a new purchase.
- The machine will be more versatile if it will do zigzag as well as straight stitch. All modern machines do.

- A smoothly graded control on the zigzag or width control is preferable to one that is 'stepped'.
- Any automatic patterns are a bonus and not absolutely necessary, although it will be seen that these can be useful and fun.
- The top tension should be easily and reliably adjustable. The tension wheels which run through the machine at the top, rather than on a screw mechanism on the front, are generally better (these are usual on up-to-date machines).
- It should be easy to adjust the bobbin tension by means of a screw on the casing, or, preferably, there should be a separate bobbin casing with a tension screw. (It should be noted that many interesting embroidery techniques are done without any tension work so this need only be taken into consideration when purchasing a new machine and not when considering whether an old machine is suitable.)
- It is better if the bobbin casing is easy to dismantle and reassemble as this is the area where any rogue threads can be caught when machining – although many machines can be cleared of bits of thread by pulling at the offending thread and rocking the mechanism to and fro. Ask in the shop how easy this is on the machine you are considering.
- The machine must have a control to lower the feed dog, or a plate to cover it for free machine embroidery (the former is preferable, as the latter leaves a small bump).
- The more robust the machine, the better. Bear in mind that for normal sewing the machine sews a seam and then rests while the next seam is being prepared; with machine embroidery the machine could be running constantly for hours, having only the same rests as the embroiderer!

The right ideas

The other essentials for machine embroidery are, of course, good design ideas. Work from drawings or develop ideas through worksheets and samples, or for a simple start try a few experiments working from photographs. Design ideas may emerge when you are sampling techniques, but always work ideas out thoroughly in worksheet or sketchbook form before going ahead with a huge project. It can be very disappointing when an idea that seemed crystal clear in your head does not work out in reality. Such an idea generally does not succeed because it was not defined clearly enough, and as soon as work commences areas of misjudgement and uncertainty start to emerge. A small amount of paperwork and some rough (or preferably neat!) sketches will clarify the thoughts and final image required and enable a successful piece of embroidery to come to fruition.

In each section of the book different ideas for designs and projects are explored or suggested using the different aspects of machine embroidery. Thus it is hoped that this book will prove helpful as a design ideas book as well as a technical course.

1

Decorative Work with Set Stitches

It is important to understand the basics of your machine before embarking on machine embroidery. The handbook will give instructions on where to find the oiling points, how to adjust top and bottom tensions, how to change stitch width and length, as well as how to use any extras such as automatic patterns or accessories. For example, oiling the bobbin race during continuous stretches of work is important and the instructions will describe how this is done and how frequently.

Understanding and mastering tension

Machine manufacturers now realize the importance of the sewing machine as a tool for creative and formal embroidery, but unfortunately this is a message that has not seeped through to many suppliers. Too often the purchaser of a new machine is informed that the tension controls must not be touched. This is probably brought about through a lack of understanding in customers who, having changed the tension on the machine for a certain purpose and, failing to reset the tension for normal sewing, return to the sewing machine shop to get it reset. My aim in the following section is to ensure that enough is understood about correct tension so that after any alterations have been made for whatever purpose the correct tension for ordinary sewing can be reset without any problems. It should also be borne in mind that if the machine is going to be left for periods of time in between use the tension should always be set correctly after use to ensure that difficulties are not encountered through forgetting what tension was last used.

In order to obtain the correct overall tension when using machine embroidery threads it is often necessary to reduce the top tension a little in order to get a good appearance, and also to prevent excessive thread breakage with these softer threads (although the amount of thread breakage experienced varies from one type of thread to another). Remember that altering the tension does not hurt the machine, and it may be necessary to adjust machine tensions often if different threads and fabrics are being used, although many modern machines have automatic self-adjustment within small margins.

It is easy to appreciate from the diagram showing thread tensions that a correct tension is easier to obtain when a good thickness of fabric is put together, so if one thickness of fabric is chosen for embroidery purposes the tensions will have to be set up very carefully. Practise by using the same type of machine embroidery thread on the top of the machine and in the bobbin. Start with a cotton thread as this is strongest and does not have a tendency towards uncontrolled thread spool-off. (Some metallic and rayon threads are apt to reel off the spool and get caught around the base of the spool holder – a condition that can be improved with a silky or metallic thread holder, which can be bought to suit a number of sewing machines.)

Experiment 1

- Set up the machine using a cotton thread on the top and a different-coloured cotton thread in the bobbin so that the effect of any adjustments in the tension can be clearly seen. Start on two thicknesses of calico and eventually work towards setting a good tension on a fine cotton or silk. Both tensions will have to be set a little loose for the latter.
- Experiment with stitch length – a longer stitch free from puckering is possible on coarser surfaces, although a good even tension that is not over tight will help to achieve this on finer surfaces.

Adjusting tensions

Adjusting the top tension may be all that is necessary to obtain good results, but if this does not work the bobbin tension will need to be checked. It is likely that it will seem a little loose (bobbin thread will be showing on the top surface, although beware as this could also indicate that the top tension is too tight!) as machine embroidery threads are so much finer than the ordinary sewing cottons that the bobbin is set up for. Adjust the bobbin tension correctly and reset the top tension accordingly.

Setting the top tension

Top tensions are set tighter towards a higher number or a plus sign on the dial, and looser towards a lower number or a minus sign. On machines using numbers, 5 is considered average and 3–4 generally has a symbol indicating the preferred tension for satin stitch and buttonholes.

Setting the bobbin tension

On a machine with a horizontal bobbin race, such as New Home and most Elna machines, there is often a screw mechanism with coloured marks which show where the

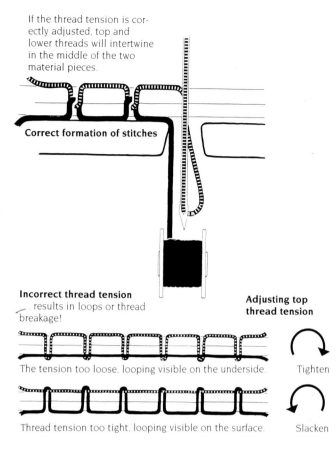

If the thread tension is correctly adjusted, top and lower threads will intertwine in the middle of the two material pieces.

Correct formation of stitches

Incorrect thread tension results in loops or thread breakage!

Adjusting top thread tension

The tension too loose, looping visible on the underside.

Tighten

Thread tension too tight, looping visible on the surface.

Slacken

Correct adjustment of tension.

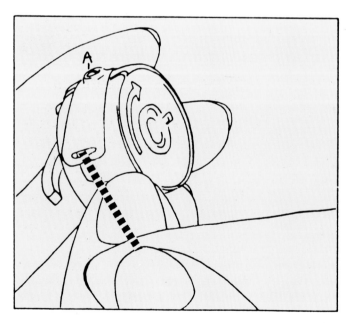

The removable bobbin case on a vertical race machine. The bobbin tension can be adjusted by turning screw A anti-clockwise to loosen, clockwise to tighten. The bobbin should turn in the direction of the arrow when unwinding.

tension will be correctly set. Again, the higher the number the tighter the tension. Very incorrect tensions can be adjusted by a screw on the side of some horizontal bobbin races, but this should only be tried after all other possibilities have been exhausted because of difficulties in resetting.

Machines with a vertical bobbin race such as Bernina, Pfaff and Husqvana Viking are somewhat easier to gauge and can be adjusted as necessary to suit any thickness of yarn. Thread the bobbin case as normal and then suspend the bobbin case by holding the thread in one hand. The case should be held over the other hand in order to catch the bobbin if it should fall out, or if the tension is too loose the case will fall. For a correct tension the case should not drop when held in this way, and the thread should barely run through when the hand suspending it makes the motion of a small sharp tap. To tighten the bobbin tension turn the screw (a) in a clockwise direction; to loosen, turn it anti-clockwise.

If you have a presser foot pressure regulator turning this down will improve the stitch result on fine fabrics – see your handbook for details.

Machine settings

Stitch: Straight.
Length: As long as possible, 3–4.
Presser foot: Zigzag or ordinary sewing foot that will hold the quilting guide.
Thread: Machine embroidery cotton no. 50.
Tension: Normal.
Needle: 70 or 80.
Note: It is essential that the threads are held firmly towards the back of the machine for the first few stitches. If not, the needle may become unthreaded, but more importantly the bobbin thread will not be under tension and there will be a resulting 'knitting' on the underside of the work.

If the needle position is up when you start you will need to allow a little slack in the top thread or the needle may hit the cover plate and break because it is being pulled out of line.

Holding the threads is not essential on some of the latest computerized machines, but it is a useful practice to adopt as other tension and more exacting techniques may require this.

Project 1

- Set up a perfect tension with as long a stitch as possible (although not a tacking stitch, should the machine have this capability).
- Machine rows of straight stitch. Try equidistant rows using the edge of the foot as a guide or by using the quilting guide. This is generally placed into a hole in the back of one of the feet and a screw holds it in place – check the handbook. The guide can then be adjusted to the desired width and lined up with previous rows of stitching to make lines perfectly equidistant, whether straight or curved.
- Try varying the distances between rows.
- Try wavy rows, or zigzagged rows.

Samples from Project 1. From top, left to right a) Rows of straight stitch with a slightly tight tension on satin fabric, laced with hand embroidery threads. b) Rows of straight stitches on cotton, laced with hand threads. c) Haphazard rows of straight stitching, laced freely (by Roma Edge.) From bottom left d) Grid of straight stitching in variegated thread. e) As d) but closer together. f) Straight stitching, forward and reverse, over a patterned fabric.

- Make regular or irregular grids.
- The stitches can now form a base for hand embroidery – large machine stitches can be particularly useful for interlace stitches that are normally associated with running stitch. Try doing these formally and informally using hand embroidery threads and a tapestry needle (a blunt fine needle is easiest).
- Try experimenting with a slightly tight top tension on shiny fabric; the slight pulling can be attractive.
- Try working in forward and in reverse over patterned or appliquéd fabric.

Working with width control stitches

A zigzag stitch or satin stitch is controlled by changing the stitch width control. How open or closed the stitch will be is governed by the stitch length control. This will be clearly marked in the handbook.

Wider satin stitches can cause the fabric to pleat – place a finger each side of the presser foot and pull widthways, or put paper under the fabric which can be torn away after sewing. Adjusting the top to a slightly looser tension can improve the appearance of satin stitch, making it look rounder.

Each time you wish to use a satin stitch, set it up by the method described below until you are completely familiar with the correct stitch length to use for different threads. Different thread thicknesses will cause a variation in the optimum stitch length.

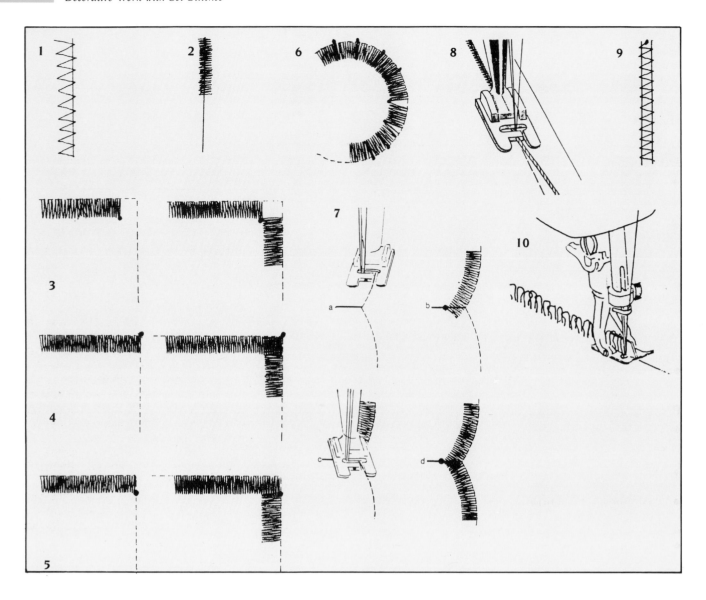

1 When applying with an open zigzag the needle should go into the background fabric as close as possible to the applied fabric. The stitching appears to be solely on the applied fabric.

2 When applying with a satin stitch the edge of the applied fabric can run along the centre of the foot, the needle zigzagging equally into the applied and background fabric. This is easier to make neat than an open zigzag.

3 Open corner: sew until a space the width of a stitch is left at the corner, place the needle on the inside edge, turn and continue sewing.

4 Closed oversewn corner: sew to the corner, put the needle in the fabric at the outer edge, lift presser foot and turn work. Lower foot and continue sewing. (It may be necessary to help a little by pushing with fingers near to the foot.)

5 Closed corner: this is probably the neatest, but a little more complicated. Sew to corner and leave the needle in the fabric in the position indicated by the dot. Lift presser foot, turn work, replace foot. Turn the needle forward by hand to lift needle, and move fabric (by lifting foot) to replace the needle into exactly the same hole. The needle is now on the right of its zigzag and sewing can continue.

6 Although it is possible to sew round wide curves by moving the fabric under the foot, if too tight a curve is attempted in this manner, the fabric will distort. To stitch a tight curve, leave the needle in the outside of the curve as often as necessary, lift foot, turn the fabric a little, replace foot, continue sewing. If the needle is left on the inside of the curve there will be a gap in the stitching.

7 The stitching of a scalloped edge.

8 When a very fine cord is to be applied it can be threaded through the hole in the cording foot. For coarser cords or ribbons place it over the front bar of the foot and guide under the needle. Stitch a straight line down the centre of the cord or ribbon or use an open zigzag. A closed zigzag over a cord will give a padded satin stitch. For a thick cord page 26.

9 An open zigzag over ribbon. Start with a few straight stitches on the ribbon so that it stays in place.

10 Using a tailor's tacking foot. If you use an open zigzag stitch the material can be manipulated fairly easily and loops stitched over a fabric; or use a satin stitch for a heavy fringe.

Machine settings

Stitch: Zigzag.
Length: Medium to short.
Width: Medium to wide.
Thread: Machine embroidery thread.
Tension: Bobbin – normal. Top – normal to slightly loose.
Needle: 80.

Experiment 2

- Try machining a line with the width set on 2. Adjust the stitch length from 4 downwards. Adjust the width control and compare the results.
- Now make a satin stitch. Select a stitch width (a medium width is easiest in the first instance), and use a firm calico fabric. Set the stitch length at 1 and gradually reduce this until the fabric is running through the machine and each thread is lying against its neighbour. Do this without pushing or pulling with your hands – the fabric should feed through completely unaided. If the fabric bunches up under the foot the stitch length is too low; if the threads are not touching each other to make an attractive satin stitch the stitch length is too high.
- Having set a perfect satin stitch, experiment with the width control.

Project 2

- Try making adjoining rows of satin stitch – this is particularly effective with a shaded or multicoloured thread.
- Make rows of satin stitch side by side, adjusting the widths as they are made.
- Make grids with narrow or wide satin stitch and use these as a base for hand work.
- Make groups of satin stitch blocks.
- Try applying ribbons, cords or thicker yarns by feeding them under the presser foot and catching them with a zigzag.
- Apply small pieces of fabric, each with a satin stitch block.
- Work a raised satin stitch by placing a cord under the presser foot and working over it.
- Try forward and reverse with a zigzag stitch.
- Try satin stitch on various gauges of canvas. A grid can be built up on a rug canvas which can then form a base for other embroidery techniques.
- Use satin stitch as a means of appliqué. The fabric to be applied can be tacked or bonded to the base fabric and satin stitched or zigzagged into place.
- Try using zigzag or satin stitch with a tailor's tacking or fringing foot. Metallic threads give an attractive result. Remember to pull the work carefully from the machine when it is finished, holding the last few stitches between thumb and finger to avoid pulling them, or finish with a few stitches on the spot by moving the needle to one side of the foot using the needle position button on the machine should it have one. This technique must be done with a very loose top tension and when finished the threads can be left as they are or cut to give a pile – paint the back with diluted PVA glue (a clear-setting glue) to hold the stitches in place.

Project 3

(The machine settings are as for Project 2, but using automatic stitches.)

- Try experimenting with the automatic patterns available on your machine – many machines today have automatic stitches that use a forward and backward movement of the feed dog to give a variety of stitch designs.
- Try altering the motif by operating any shortening or lengthening controls, or changing stitch widths and lengths (see your handbook for guidance).
- Make rows of automatic stitches side by side.
- Try making rows of the same or different stitches over each other.
- Try mixing stitches. Change pattern after each completed pattern, or part way through a row.
- Try using automatic stitches for a free appliqué with pieces applied with bonding fabric.
- Try mixing these with hand stitches that resemble them, for example four-sided or cross stitch.
- If your machine has a memory, experiment with it: stitches can be chosen, reversed, lengthened, shortened, mixed and fed into the memory as a repeat pattern.
- Some of the latest computerized machines have facilities for designing stitches that can be used for repeat motifs. This can be useful for creating borders on pictures, or motifs for use with free machine as well as set stitch embroidery. They can be mixed with other stitches and used for borders and braids on garments and soft furnishings. Try designing your own stitches if your machine has this facility.
- Remember that although many automatic stitches can look mundane or frivolous on the machine diagrams, they can become creative and interesting when used with imagination.

Page 14

Examples of Project 2. Top left to bottom left a) Grid in ecru satin stitch, hand stitched crosses. b) Grid in satin stitch on raw ecru silk, green hand satin stitch. c) Satin stitch, changing the width control slowly, then quickly; open zigzag over ribbon; padded satin stitch worked over a cord. A variegated thread is used throughout. Top right to bottom right d) Satin stitch blocks on background, and applying pieces of net, worked in a variegated thread. Net applied with a satin stitch. e) Satin stitch over coarse rug canvas, stitched onto a ground of nets with a cross stitch – an idea based on fishing nets. f) Fringes worked with the tailor's tacking foot.

Page 15

Examples of Project 3. Top left to bottom left a) Examples of automatic stitches, open and closed. b) Two stitches alternated in the memory. c) Automatic stitches with hand stitched cross and herringbone. Top right to bottom right d) Rows of stitches with an elongated triangle worked singly at the base. e) Appliqué using bonding fabric and automatic stitches. f) An archway design put into the computer and then manipulated, elongated, mirrored, reverse stitches included between each repeat, mirrored alternate stitches, a flower design put into the computer. (All samples worked on a Pfaff Creative 1473 machine.)

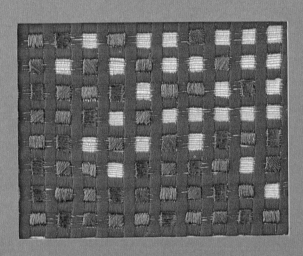

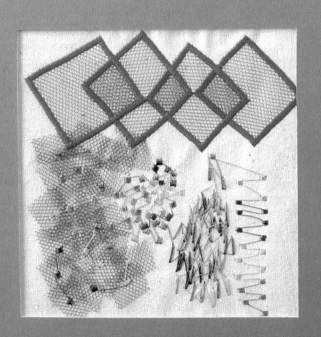

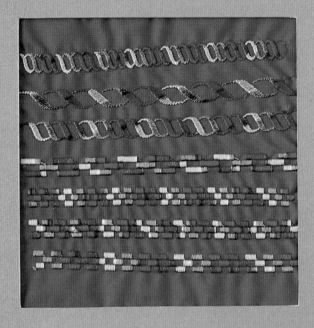

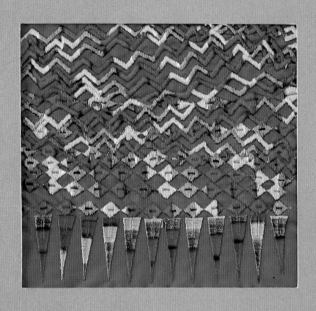

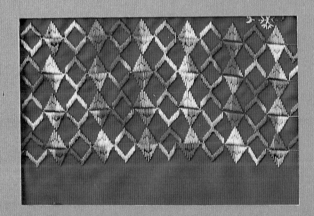

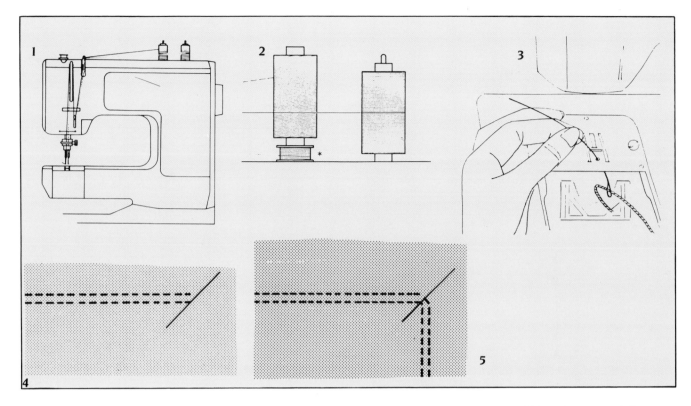

1 Threading for a twin needle.
2 Bobbins for a triple needle; continue to thread as for twin needle with righthand threads doubling up.
3 Use of fine wire to thread a cord through the hole in the footplate. Some machines have an attachment which fits onto the front of the cover plate through which the cord is threaded.
4/5 Sewing corners. Right-angle or tighter corners cannot be turned in one stitch – work as follows (the diagonal line is a visual aid): sew until the inner needle is on the line; using the hand wheel bring the needle into the work, taking down and partially up again until the eyes are just visible and the tips still in the fabric, turn half way round the corner; using the handwheel make one stitch, bringing the needles to the same position. Complete the turn and continue sewing.

Using twin and triple needles

Many decorative effects can be created using twin and triple needles. For the following techniques you will need a variety of needles: twin in sizes 1.6mm, 2mm, 3mm, and 4mm; also one triple needle – these come in 3mm only. For decorative stitching a zigzag foot will be needed, for pintucking or corded pintucking choose a grooved pintucking foot. Threading up the machine is very straightforward, just be careful that the threads do not get tangled and follow the diagram. Threads can be the same colour, shades of the same colour, or completely different colours – experiment with your own combinations.

Machine settings

Stitch: Straight stitch.
Length: Medium to short.
Presser foot: Grooved pintucking foot.
Thread: Machine embroidery cotton.
Tension: Normal to tight.
Needle: Twin needle, various widths.

Grooved pintucking feet should be chosen as follows: 3 groove – heavy fabrics; 5 groove – medium fabrics; 7 groove – fine to medium fabrics; 9 groove – fine fabrics such as lawn and silk. The wider the needle used the larger will be the pintuck made, although very wide needles do not work well on fine fabrics. A tighter tension will make the pintuck look more like one done in the traditional 'pleating' fashion.

A shorter stitch length will also help to create a deeper pintuck.

Project 4

- Experiment with different fabrics, different stitch lengths, and different tensions to create pintucks.
- Try stitching rows of pintucks as close as possible. (The previous pintuck is placed in one of the grooves of the foot when the next pintuck is made.) Stitch rows a little further apart – use the side of the foot as a guide.
- Stitch rows at varying distances – use the quilting guide.
- Try free and formal smocking on these samples.
- Stitch rows of pintucks in one direction, then stitch over them at right angles, going first in one direction and then the other to flatten the pintucks in alternate directions.

Samples from Project 4. Top left and right a) and b) Worked on calico with a layer of patterned fabric under; the fabric is pintucked and the top layer snipped away in places (by Liza Collyer). Left to right c) Pintucks on calico, smocked by hand. d) (top) Pintucks crossing at right angles, worked on the cross of the fabric. e) Straight lines of pintucks, then stitched over on the cross, the fabric is slightly pulled. f) Straight lines, worked over at right angles, first in one direction, then the other.

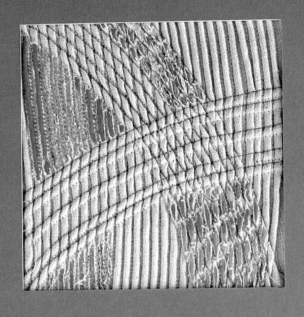

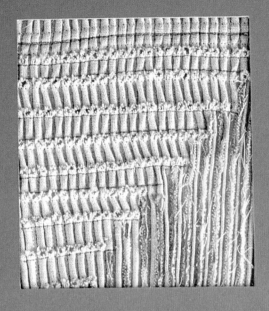

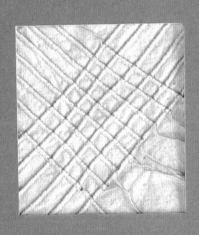

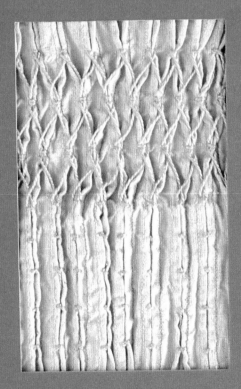

- Over straight rows of pintucks stitch another on the cross of the fabric. If the fabric is pulled in the direction of the stitching when the work is done on the cross the pintucks will pull out of shape into curls.
- Try doing this over the cross in both directions.
- Experiment with fabrics – dyed, patterned, silks, panne velvet, layered see-through fabrics, etc.
- Pintuck on two layers of fabric (a patterned or dyed fabric could be used underneath) and then slash through the pintucks to reveal the second fabric.
- Pintucks could be worked in waves or follow a design with corners (see diagram on page 16).
- Try pintucking with a cord or gimp – this can be used to follow a design and give an effect similar to Italian quilting, or used for ordinary pintucking. The cord is either threaded through the cover plate (see diagram on page 16) or guided into place through a plate which can be fixed to the cover plate. (See your machine handbook for guidelines.) Ensure that the gimp will run smoothly and use a 2mm twin needle as this tends to be the maximum width any thread that will thread through the guide hole will require. If too large a needle width is chosen the cord will not fit well and the resulting tuck will be untidy.

Decorative stitch techniques can also be interesting with a twin or triple needle. Even rows of satin or zigzag stitching can be attractive, but try using automatic patterns. Needles of any width can be used, and their relative spacings can produce remarkable differences in the nature of the finished work.

Machine settings

Stitch: Select zigzag or automatic patterns.
Length: To suit pattern.
Width: To suit pattern and needle.
Thread: Machine embroidery.
Tension: Normal to loose.
Needle: Twin and triple, various sizes.
Note: Care should be taken when selecting stitch width. The maximum stitch width setting on a machine allows a single needle to work the design without hitting the cover plate or foot, so make sure a twin or triple needle will not be broken by stitching the whole of a chosen design – up to the most extreme width – by turning the hand wheel. Turn the stitch width down appropriately so that the needles no longer touch the sides of the presser foot. Remember to do this whenever you are resetting to a new design. Some electronic machines have a twin needle button which automatically adjusts any decorative stitches so that they are suitable for use with a 3mm twin or triple needle – check the handbook.

Project 5

- Try zigzag and satin stitches with different needle widths, using toning or contrasting colours in the needles.
- Try a selection of automatic stitches, including ones based on satin and running stitches – again try a selection of needles.
- Mix the above with pintucking or corded pintucks.
- Try varying the designs and stitches as in Project 2.
- Try using dyed or patterned fabric.

Samples from Project 5. Left Pintucks and automatic stitches using contrasting colours (Bernina machine by Terry Waglan). Right Twin and triple needle samples of automatic stitches. The Rhodes key design has the reverse side shown next to it. (Worked on a Pfaff machine.)

Corded twin needle worked to create a trellis design. Top Layers of organdie and transparent fabrics, stitched with a gold thread, the top layer being black. Diamonds are cut through a different number of layers to reveal the appropriate colour. Bottom Metallic dyes applied with a potato print, then stitched. Worked on silk noile. (Bernina.)

2
Working with the Darning Foot

It is a good idea to try your first steps in free machine embroidery using a darning foot as it has many advantages:

- The novice may feel that the fingers are better protected.
- It is essential that the foot mechanism is lowered even when a foot is not being used (otherwise the top tension is not engaged), and using a darning foot obviates this simple mistake.
- Fabrics do not have to be stretched tightly when using a darning foot.
- It is easier to stitch quilted or bonded fabrics.
- Designs may flow across the fabric more easily as embroidery rings do not have to be used if the fabric is stiff.
- The fabric will have to be stiff or robust enough to manipulate by hand and not be wrinkled up by the machining process; if this is difficult an embroidery ring can be used.
- It is easier to stitch on heavily stitched or worked areas, glued appliqué, canvas embroidery etc.

The disadvantages can be seen when making comparisons with working completely without a foot (which for ease of manipulation almost always has to be done in an embroidery hoop):

- Even if the darning foot is replaced with a free machine embroidery foot (although this is not so useful when working without a ring), it is still impossible to see all of the embroidery being worked.
- Detail and accuracy can be difficult if the whole of the immediate embroidery cannot be seen – particularly exacting lines which may be necessary for some patterns, or writing, or for drawing faces.
- The darning foot may also get caught on areas of threads, changes in texture, or any other bumps which have already been added to the surface of the embroidery (such as beads or hand stitches).

On balance it will be seen that there are some areas of free machine embroidery where the darning foot is the ideal tool, and other techniques where it is better to work entirely free.

Most sewing machines include a darning foot in the accessory box. It is usually a small hoop – less than 1cm (½in) across – and has a mechanism which helps it to 'bounce', yet firmly hold the fabric it is sewing when the needle is about to enter. This mechanism will either be an arm which fits against the needle screw, or the foot itself

will be spring-loaded and floating. With some machines (such as the Pfaff) it is possible to use the foot holder alone as well as or instead of the foot provided.

For free machine embroidery it is also necessary to lower the feed dog of the machine, change the cover plate, or add a feed cover plate to the existing plate. (The darning section in the handbook will explain how to do this on your machine.) A machine that lowers the feed dog is easiest to use as the bump caused by a cover plate can catch awkwardly on the fabric, or can cause the fabric to be held too loosely when using an embroidery hoop and no foot.

Machine settings

Stitch: Straight.
Length: 0 (when working free machine embroidery you control the stitch length by moving the frame).
Thread: Machine embroidery thread – use cotton or good quality rayon as this will be easiest.
Tension: Normal. (It may be necessary to loosen the top tension slightly to obtain a 'normal' tension with free machine embroidery.)
Needle: 80. Use a ballpoint needle when working on quilt wadding.
Feed dog: Lowered or covered – consult your handbook.
Remember that you are in control of the fabric – if you do not move it, the stitches will be all on one spot. You can move the fabric as much as you like but small stitches are easier to start with as the needle and thread are less likely to break. Run the machine at a medium speed as smoothly as possible and move the fabric fairly slowly – create a line of thread rather than concentrating on individual stitches. Remember that the fabric or frame can be moved in any direction – forwards, backwards, from side to side – stitches do not always have to come towards you. (This sounds obvious but it is a common mistake when stitching 'free' for the first time.)

Remember to hold the threads to the back of the work when starting off to prevent thread tangle. If the first few stitches are made into the same hole, and the last few finished off in the same way, the threads can usually be cut (although additional precautions may be appropriate on some garments or soft furnishings).

Experiment 3

First become familiar with free machine embroidery using a darning foot. Use calico stretched tightly in a wooden

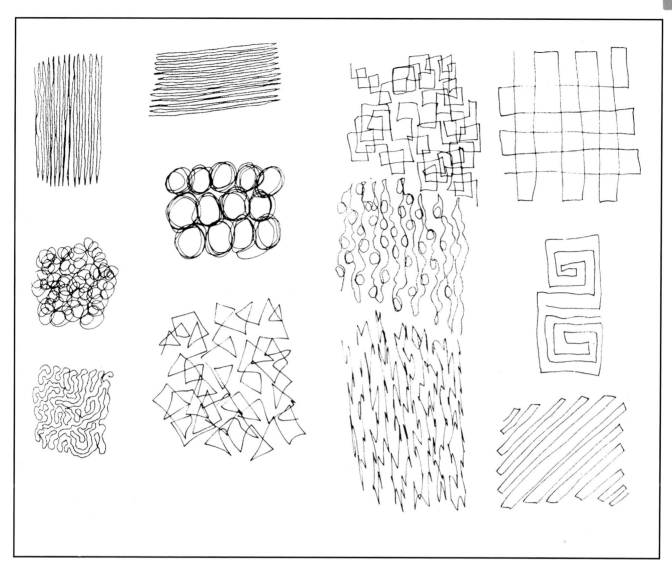

Marks suitable for Experiment 3.

hoop or attached to a heavyweight fabric stiffener. See chapter 3 for the best method of holding an embroidery hoop – note that the hoop is held the other way up to that normally used for hand stitching, with the fabric touching the bed of the machine.

- Draw rows of straight lines side by side using small stitches by moving the fabric backwards and forwards.
- Draw rows of straight lines from side to side by moving the ring from left to right.
- Try each of the above, varying the speed of the machine and the speed at which the fabric is moved to achieve a variety of stitch lengths. If the bobbin thread shows each time the direction is changed this can be improved by loosening the top tension, or slightly tightening the bobbin tension.
- Try drawing circles, squares and any other patterns and movements that come to mind.

If you are not using a hoop the fabric should be taut and be held by fingers pressing on the machine bed each side of the darning foot. Alternatively, the fabric can be firmly held by the edges in order to move it, but it must be held down on the machine bed.

Project 6

- Make up a sandwich for quilting. This should comprise: first, a fabric suitable for the surface (shiny fabrics respond well to this technique); then a quilt wadding – most commonly available in polyester in a variety of thicknesses or weights, but also obtainable in wool (domette) or silk; and third, a base fabric, which can be a soft or stiff muslin, or cotton fabric such as calico. The sandwich is made by tacking an upright cross from the centre of the fabric outwards, then tacking another cross at 45 degrees to the first one. If the piece to be quilted is larger than 50cm (20in) a grid should be tacked at about 5–10cm (2–4in) intervals.
- The top fabric could be treated in a number of ways – try silk dyes treated with salt, spongeing, spray dye, by masking areas and splattering with a toothbrush, printing with potatoes or other objects, or simply drawing on the pattern to be quilted.

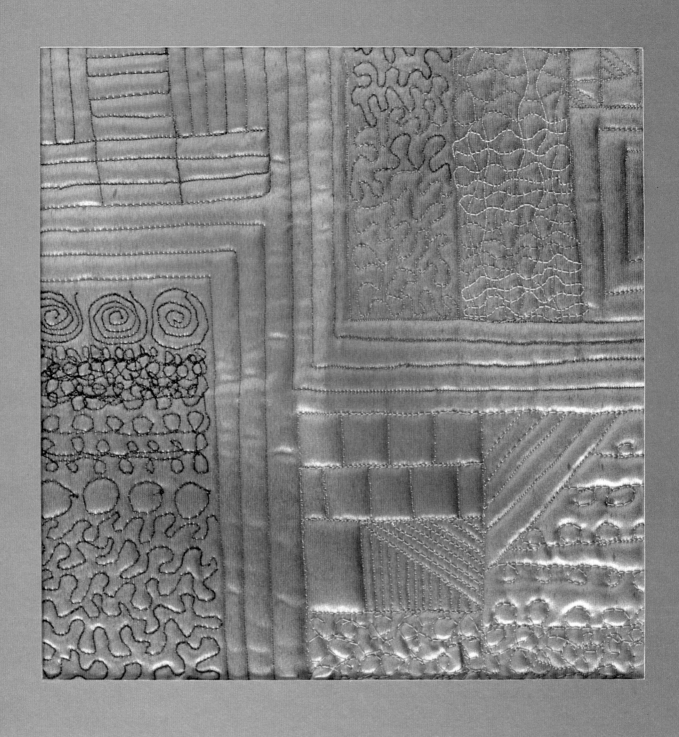

Sample of stitches worked in a variety of threads on a spray-dyed quilted satin. (Worked on a Bernina machine by Kay Bragg.)

- Work free quilting over the surface of the fabric without an embroidery ring. The dyeing may inspire the lines of the quilting, suggesting flowing lines or quilting concentrated in one or two areas, otherwise a drawn-on design may help.
- Try using variegated or metallic threads.

Cushion cover worked on quilted habutai silk using silk dyes and resist. Each square is outlined in its own colour thread; a slight glint of gold can be seen as the top tension is a little tight and is pulling through the gold bobbin thread (see chapter 4). The cord is worked with an open zigzag over a collection of threads, with a machined satin stitch over the corner where the two cords meet to make a tassel.

23

Machine settings

Stitch: Straight or zigzag.

Length: Set on 0.

Width: 0 to wide.

Thread: Machine embroidery plus others for applying or cords.

Tension: Normal.

Needle: 80 (or 90–100 if using rougher metallic threads; the smooth metallic threads will run happily through an 80 needle).

Note: For information on creating a good free satin stitch see the section on working with zigzag stitches, chapter 3 (page 38).

Pot plant worked in bonded silks to a silk noile background. The ribbons are applied as described in chapter 1 (page 12). Straight stitches and open and closed zigzag are used on the pot, leaves and flowers. Each fabric piece has at least a few stitches to hold it in place, but these are done freely to lighten the quality of the work. (Bernina.)

Project 7

- Cut out a quantity of fabrics that have been applied to bonding fabric. Choose harmonious or contrasting colours. Cut out shapes that will go well together – for example, collections of geometric shapes, curves or circles, or flame shapes.
- Design a picture and work this in appliqué.

Archways. *Worked on fine lockweave canvas with free machine embroidery using a darning foot and automatic stitches with feed and normal foot. Hand stitches are worked first in some areas and machining added. In other areas the machining is worked first and the hand stitches worked into or round it. Pieces of metallized plastic are appliquéed. The large zigzag at the top of the picture is worked with a wide machine zigzag freehand. (Bernina and Pfaff.)*

- If working freely, bond the shapes neatly or haphazardly onto a firm surface – you can build up the patterns and ideas as you go. Work over the surface of the shapes with a free straight stitch, or use zigzag and satin stitch. Remember that you cannot select a stitch length. The stitch width selector operates when working with free machine embroidery, but if you wish to choose between a zigzag or satin stitch it is the speed at which you move the fabric that will make the difference.

Project 8

- Try working with the darning foot on canvas. Choose a 'lockweave' or 'interlock' canvas otherwise the threads will be drawn together and the result will be a sort of pulled work. Try stitching over the surface of the canvas with straight stitch, zigzag and satin stitch.
- Try applying pieces of fabric to canvas, either using the darning foot in a free way, or using normal sewing techniques.
- Try hand stitching onto the canvas and then working into this by machine.
- Try working by machine, deliberately leaving gaps which can then have hand stitches worked into them.

Samples from Project 9. Left Pieces of thread offcuts and net applied to a patterned fabric surface with satin stitch blocks. Right Piping cords wrapped with a satin stitch and applied to a fabric with an open zigzag (red metallic); a large zigzag was then selected for the freer gold stitching. (Pfaff Creative 1473.)

Project 9

The darning foot can also be useful when applying threads, bits and pieces of unbonded fabric, or applying cords or wrapping them:

- Cut short lengths of interesting yarns – hand embroidery or knitting yarns – or pieces of offcut machine thread. Place them onto a fabric surface and stitch over them using a darning foot. (This may be easier if the work is placed in a hoop to hold the fabric taut and flat.) The threads can jump about and catch on the darning foot, but simply cut the darning foot free if it becomes trapped. Threads can be held in place with a cocktail stick if necessary.
- Cut fabric into small pieces – use harmonious, contrasting or toning colours. Their position on the surface could be used to build up a picture or pattern, and they may be glued on, or apply a little bonding fabric to each one, or stitch each piece down with a satin stitch block before adding any further stitching to enhance the design or put them under a transparent fabric.

- Try wrapping cords by threading them through or under the darning foot (*through* for fine cords, *under* for thicker ones) and under the needle. Because you are in control of stitch length, wrapping can vary between being open or a satin stitch covering the cords completely. The cord to be wrapped could be made out of a selection of threads rather than one cord, and the variety of threads can be left exposed where a more open zigzag is worked. Hold the cord in the left hand to the back of the machine and guide with the right hand in front of the needle, stretching the cord tightly in between. The width control should be set so that the needle enters the machine on each side of the cord without touching it, thus wrapping it. The thickness of the cord that can be wrapped by the machine will therefore be dependent on how wide a zigzag the machine can do.
- Try applying lengths of cord – try some you have wrapped, to build up an intricate and textured surface. They could, for example, be laid side by side, in trellises or grids, or cut into small bunches and applied. Further hand stitches or small tassels and beads could be added to make an even richer surface. An independent trellis or net could be made by stitching cords together in a grid structure.

Worksheet of clothing ideas for laid grounds of machine-made cords.

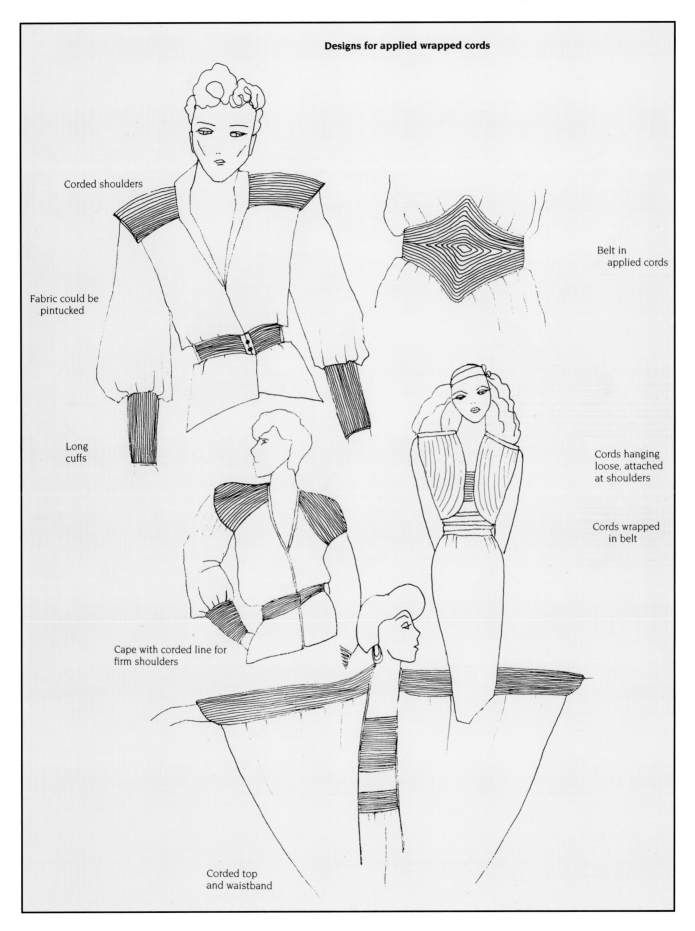

Designs for applied wrapped cords

Corded shoulders

Fabric could be pintucked

Long cuffs

Cape with corded line for firm shoulders

Corded top and waistband

Belt in applied cords

Cords hanging loose, attached at shoulders

Cords wrapped in belt

Panel or cushion cover worked on quilted silk crepe. The satin stitches are worked with the foot on and the feed in place, the remainder is straight and vermicelli stitch worked with a darning foot. The centre of the flower is corded whip stitch (see chapter 4). (Bernina machine with the 6mm zigzag worked on the Pfaff machine.)

Free Machine Embroidery

It is possible to use a darning foot for the following techniques, but it is wise to practise without as it is so much easier to see all of the embroidery at once without a foot (even a free embroidery foot). Most of the techniques can be practised with the hands placed on the embroidery hoop – it is only in areas of heavy stitching that it will be necessary to bring the first or first and second fingers in close to the work.

An embroidery hoop is necessary when working without a foot, as it is essential to keep the work stretched drum-tight. With a little practice it is possible to do this with your fingers with some fabrics, but manipulation becomes more difficult without the use of a hoop. An embroidery hoop is used upside-down to the way it would be used for hand embroidery. It is also best to choose a wooden hoop, and the rings can be bound for increased grip, although this is not absolutely necessary. A metal and plastic hoop does not hold the work as tightly and will hardly work at all for heavily stitched embroidery or quilting.

It is important to use a good hand position for machine embroidery. I have found the following to be most successful because it gives control for all types of stitching with only a slight variation in the grip (see diagram below). The ring is held firmly between the thumb and second finger, thus the thumb can push the ring away from you, the second finger can push the work towards you, and working together they give perfect control in forwards and backwards motions. Use the index finger exactly in between, placed against the inside of the ring, 'pushing' towards the outside. Now, with both hands in position (make sure your arms are supported comfortably), the two index fingers will have complete control over widthwise movements by pushing and pulling against each other. Any stitch patterns

can now be created easily and accurately. It sounds very technical – and daunting – that you have to think of so many movements at once, but, like driving a car or riding a bicycle, it becomes second nature in no time.

Machine settings

Stitch: Straight.
Length: Set on 0.
Width: Set on 0.
Thread: Experiment with a variety of machine embroidery threads.
Tension: Normal (it may be necessary to loosen the top tension to achieve this).
Foot: No foot, but remember to put down the lever in order to engage the top tension.
Feed: Lowered or covered (see handbook).
Needle: 80.
Fabric: In embroidery hoop.

The main problems and their solutions

Tangle when starting off

Hold the threads for the first few stitches to ensure that the bobbin thread is under tension; if necessary bring the threads through to the top.

The foot lever may have been left in the up position – the foot must be brought down to engage the top tension. This is a common error that even the most experienced embroiderers make from time to time. To avoid it either consciously keep the foot position down instead of up whenever you are working without a foot, or adopt the habit of going through the motions of lowering the foot just before you are to start stitching; you will thus feel whether the lever has been put down or not.

Failure to make stitches

Here the machine stitches but does not pick up the bobbin thread. First check that there is thread on the bobbin! But, assuming this to be in order, the problem invariably arises because the fabric is not stretched tightly enough in the hoop – it must be drum-tight. Quilt waddings or many thicknesses of bonding or stitching can cause the fabric to bounce and the stitches not to catch. If this is the reason, bring the first and second fingers (or first only) into the ring

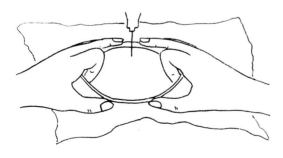

Hand position on embroidery hoop. Note that the fabric is 'upside-down' from the normal hand embroidery position.

close to the needle and press firmly; alternatively use a darning foot

Needle or top thread breaks when starting off

This is because the top thread is being held too tightly for those first few stitches. Whilst holding the bobbin firmly, it is necessary to allow a little slack on the top thread. If this proves impossible to master, solve the problem by starting all stitching with the needle in the work, and hold the threads firmly. Also check that threading is correct.

Thread breaks during sewing

It may be that the stitches were too large and the material was being pulled when the machine thread take-up lever was not in the correct position. Practise smaller stitches by increasing the machine speed and decreasing the speed at which you move the ring. If you wish to make longer stitches you can gradually master this as the sound and rhythm of the machine become more familiar.

If the thread seems to break on the top of the machine whilst machining, it may be that the top tension is too tight. If the thread frays or gets caught refer to the section on difficult threads. If the thread seems to be catching and breaking in the bobbin area of the machine it may be that the top thread is too loose, so check for looping on the underside of the fabric which would indicate this and reset the tensions.

Very often this sort of problem can be caused by incorrect threading. Look hard, but it is often difficult to spot a mistake, so if nothing comes to light rethread the machine. If the problem still prevails go back to ordinary sewing with a foot and normally set tensions, then, having cured the problem, start again.

The top thread may be breaking in the bobbin area because the bobbin case has been assembled incorrectly, so if you have recently had cause to do this, check it.

Threads can also fray or break during sewing when working into already heavily worked areas. Avoid this, or choose a thread that will stand more of this sort of treatment – a cotton thread is best – or increase the needle size.

An even machine speed will help prevent thread breakage.

If none of the above solves the problem, and you have tried a new needle (the old one may be bent or blunt) then there may be something wrong with the alignment of the machine, particularly if you can also hear a knocking noise when sewing. In that case obviously the best thing to do is to have the machine serviced, but always attach a note saying where the difficulties lie so the engineer will know what to look for.

Needle breaks during sewing

It may have been bent.

The work may be too thick for the needle comfortably to pass through – use a thicker needle, or ballpoint if you are working with synthetic fabric.

The stitches that are being attempted could be too large – the needle is being pulled against the cover plate between stitches because there is not enough thread at the point at which the ring is being moved to make that size of stitch. Practise making smaller stitches. In time, when you understand fully the rhythm of the machine, larger stitches will be possible.

Using difficult threads

Using machine embroidery cottons should cause no problems whatsoever. Many people are put off using the silkier threads, however, because first encounters prove difficult. The slippery nature of rayon and metallic threads can make them more difficult to use, as well as the fact that they are less robust; and with rough metallic threads other problems can arise.

The most common problem is that the thread slips down to the bottom of the spool during machining, winds around the spool holder and this causes the thread to break. This will happen less if the machine is run at a fairly constant speed without jerky stops and starts. Also watch at the top of the work whilst sewing so you can note right away any sudden change in thread tension. If the bobbin thread should start to show the top thread has probably become caught, so stop immediately and rewind the spool correctly. Matters can also be improved by using a looser top tension than you would normally.

If the problems persist then there are a number of remedies that can be tried. Spool holders can be purchased for metallic and shiny threads for a number of machines, which help guide the thread off the middle of the spool. Then again, many people try taping a tapestry needle to the side of the machine, but this method increases the top thread tension, and gives another obstacle to thread. Others try stiff wire wound round the spool holder and made into a hook to ensure that the thread leaves the top of the spool. Nets, dairy cartons, bits of carpet, jars for the spool or even separate spool stands can all be employed. Each method has its devotees, but if you take care as suggested you should find few problems, and generally only encounter them if the rayon thread you are using is particularly loosely wound – a manufacturing fault that occurs with some brands. Otherwise my favourite method is to exchange the felt on the spool holder for carpet.

The softer threads can also fray or break more often when entering the fabric. A looser tension can help this, but they will inevitably break more easily if they pass through an area that is already heavily worked. The use of a darning foot which holds the fabric still and taut for needle entry will help, as will using a slightly larger needle (90–100); otherwise, avoid over-stitching with softer rayon and metallic threads if this seems to be a problem.

For rougher metallic threads all the above advice applies – they are particularly prone to fraying. The effects they can give make persevering worthwhile, however, so choose a loose tension, a needle size of 90 or 100, and work with a slower speed than usual to prevent the thread fraying at the needle.

With care and attention it is possible to avoid all of the problems that can affect machine embroidery, so don't be put off – it can be easy, creative and quick, and can free those inhibitions gained through years of painstaking handstitchery.

Using straight stitch

Experiment 4

- Experiment with the sort of marks that can be made with free machine embroidery – remember that the ring can be moved in any direction, and that the stitching does not have to come towards you.
- Try stitching straight lines side by side – do this slowly and carefully and gradually speed up. Make sure that all the gaps are filled with stitching. Experiment with different stitch lengths by moving the ring faster. (A shiny variegated thread will make the appearance more interesting.)
- Try working the above, but from side to side.
- Try making small blocks of straight stitch in different directions; the blocks will catch the light in different ways.
- Try drawing a shape and filling it in with neat lines side by side. A petal shape can be a good practice piece. Draw the petal with stitches, and then divide it into areas with curved lines which will indicate the curves that are to be followed for the filling stitching. If a shaded thread is to be used try to keep the darker thread towards the bottom and the lighter towards the edge of the petal; concentrate on the top thread as it reaches the needle and move to a suitable area to do the stitching as the colour changes.
- Try a 'weave' stitch. Draw a number of verticals, taking care not to make them loopy but keeping the turning points as points. Then draw a number of horizontals in the same way. The hoop movement is backwards and forwards a few times, and then side to side a few times. Move along the horizontal or vertical a little more each time to start another set of stitching. Keep working to fill or half fill in a background. This method can be used to apply fabrics and merge them into a background or one another.
- Try creating a filled background by making small overlapping circles. This will be easy if you use the hand position correctly on the ring. Also, keep the machine speed fast and the hand movement fairly slow; failure to

do this will result in triangles or squares instead of circles. These can be attractive but the thread or needle may snap more easily with this type of stitching as the stitches created are larger, so take care.

- Try drawing circles on a larger scale and re-emphasizing them; this can make a nice filling and the circles do not have to overlap.
- Draw vertical lines a little distance apart and make them 'wiggle' haphazardly. This can be achieved by moving the ring forwards and backwards, but shaking it slightly occasionally (I call it the 'drunken wiggle'). It can also be achieved by going from side to side. This works particularly well on dyed backgrounds where it can draw the eye and colour movement from one area to the next.
- Try variations on the above – small circles can be drawn as well as the 'wiggles', or, instead of making the jerking movement from side to side, make it backwards and forwards to make the line of stitching heavier in places.
- Vermicelli stitch has gained its name from its appearance. It is worked in small wiggles and curves which do not overlap or cross each other. The effect creates a useful background texture that looks particularly good when used with whip or cable stitching (see next chapter), or when used with quilting.
- Try drawing shapes – any shape. Try leaves, flowers, bricks, a stone wall, or write an alphabet or your name. Letters are easiest if each stroke is carefully worked twice, allowing the machine line to finish a letter where the next one is to begin – sometimes three strokes may be needed, but this will look better if all the lines are done with at least two strokes.
- Draw a shape and emphasize it. Try to go round the shape again exactly on the same lines as before to make the line firmer. Then try working around a shape a little more inaccurately, so that the result is more like a haphazard sketch.
- Try 'long stitch'. A long stitch can be created by moving the ring slowly and carefully in time with a slow-running machine when the needle is at its highest. Alternatively, if your machine has a tacking stitch button, the needle will make every second or fourth stitch, which allows the ring to be moved a long way thus taking up the large quantities of thread which are given by the movement of the take-up arm for the times that the needle is not in operation. Try using long stitches with shiny threads to create a nap, or use other stitches running over long stitches to create an interesting texture.

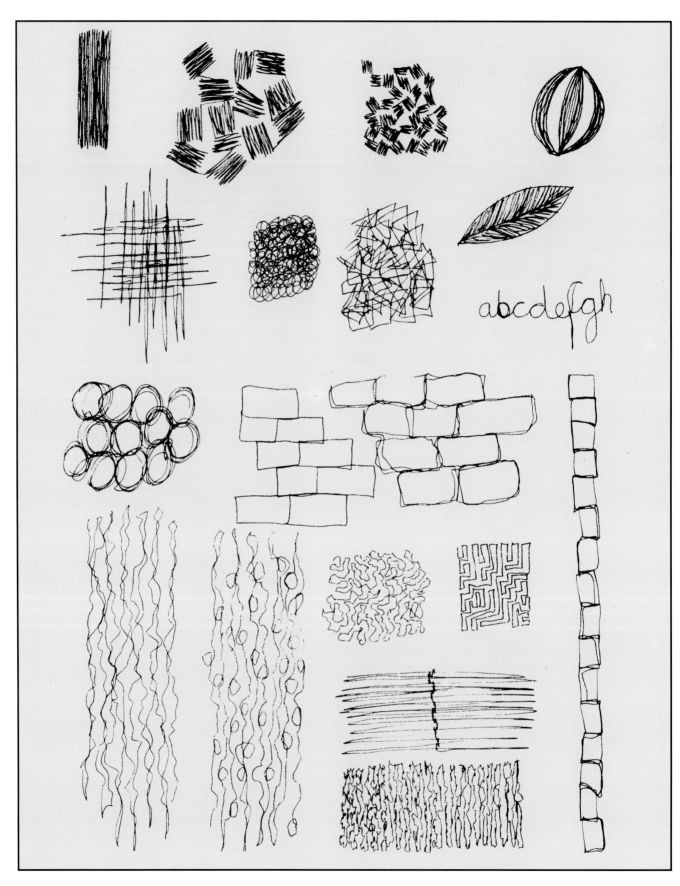

Straight stitch movements suitable for free machine embroidery designed by
drawing with a continuous line.

Examples of free machine embroidery with a straight stitch from
Experiment 4 worked with a variegated thread on calico.

Project 10

- Using the techniques already learned, make a machine drawing based on a landscape or garden subject. A photograph may be used for this, but a pen or pencil drawing would be best as the image will already be translated into linear marks which will be easier to work by machine.
- Using a photograph, water colour, pencil crayon or pastel drawing, make a machined image using coloured threads to fill in areas. Consider suitable textures for each area. As you draw for embroidery purposes, drawing becomes easier as the marks start to relate to possible embroidery stitches and patterns, and this in turn will also make the embroidery easier as the drawing will dictate which sort of stitch marks or textures to use. Many people find themselves first learning to draw through the use of the machine needle, which is somehow less intimidating than a pencil. Eventually, through learning to observe through embroidery, drawing with art materials becomes easier.
- Use fabrics bonded in some areas and blend the whole thing together with machine embroidery in suitable textures. A building site might make a suitable design source. Consider how colours can be confined to an area or used to merge one shape into the next.
- Try line drawings and fillings on dyed grounds. Choose stitches that will help to move the eye and colour from one area to another. Note that on larger pieces where an area to be filled in cannot be placed within the hoop all at once, the stitches must be 'bricked' to join neatly together, rather than stitched solidly up to the edge of the ring (see diagram below).

Rough sketch with fibre tip pen of a Cotswold country lane. A colour photograph was also taken of the scene to give colour details.

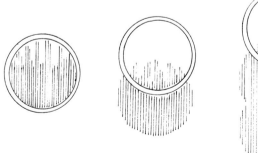

Diagram of 'bricking' large areas of machine embroidery filling worked in a ring.

Embroidery worked on a dyed ground of noile silk. from above: The sketch marks help in the interpretation of what stitch marks to use. The colours are chosen to give an autumnal feel, but only three different reels are used (one is variegated). All the stitching is straight running stitch.

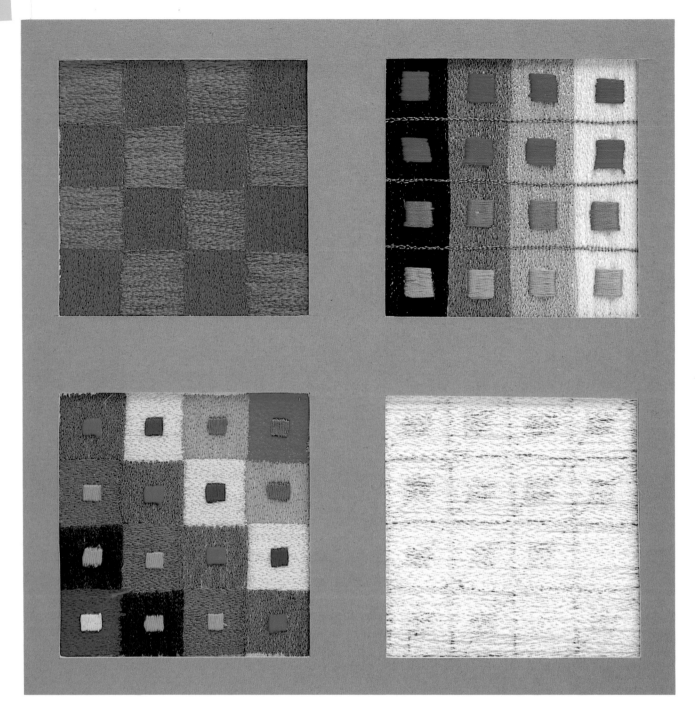

● Try colour experiments. Colour circles and colour theory can inspire many worthwhile experiments. Try stitching complementaries on top of each other: blue onto orange, red onto green, violet onto yellow. Try making tonal areas in black, grey and white, and stitching pastels and full colours over these. Try creating harmonious colour schemes or ones that clash. Try stitching warm colours over cool and vice versa.

Samples of colour work from Project 10. Top left Squares of straight-stitched blocks worked in complementary colours. Each square is stitched over a square of its complementary colour, thus adding more depth. Bottom left Straight stitch blocks of rainbow colours, each with a satin stitch block of its complementary in the centre. Note, for instance, how the purple on yellow looks small and recessed, whereas the yellow on purple looks larger and comes forward, yet they are worked in exactly the same way. Top right Four achromatic bands shaded from black to white, with four reds of different densities. Bottom right Worked completely in straight stitch, a grid with different rainbow colour blocks joined by a thread. The whole is then stitched over in white. The full colours of the blocks become pastels.

● Try drawing directly from life using the machine onto a piece of natural or dyed fabric. Choose a view from a window, or a still life placed nearby. When you are used to your machine this sort of drawing can seem remarkably easy, and encourage you to attempt to work with art materials if you are not already doing so.

Spray-dyed and potato-printed noile silk with straight stitch free embroidery. (Worked on an Elna machine by Roma Edge.)

Working with zigzag stitches

When working with straight stitches the machine length is set at 0 as this is best for the machine. With the feed dog lowered or covered it is only the operator who decides stitch length and direction, so the 0 stitch length setting makes no difference to the actual stitching. However, things are slightly different when using the zigzag and other automatic width stitches. The stitch length is still governed by moving the embroidery hoop, but the stitch width is determined by what is selected on the width control.

When embroiderers first discovered that the sewing machine could be a useful tool, swing needles were not available, and in order to create a zigzag or satin stitch the width and length had to be controlled through the careful movement of the embroidery hoop. Fortunately, swing needle machines will now create whatever width of stitch is selected, leaving the embroiderer to concentrate on stitch length and direction.

Holding the hoop correctly is particularly important when working with a zigzag stitch, as stitch length can be more crucial for an even appearance. The hand position previously described will help good control, and is also useful for when the hoop has to be held absolutely still – necessary for some of the stitch designs – or when it must be moved very slowly, as in the case of satin stitch.

To work a satin stitch hold the ring in the correct manner and place the palms of both hands firmly onto the bed of the machine. Now move the ring slowly towards or away from you to create an even stitch. Imagine that there is a battle going on between your thumb and second finger, that one wishes to push and the other is trying to keep the hoop still; working against each other in this way an evenly paced stitch length can be maintained, creating a good solid satin stitch. The stitch will look best if created in one direction only – don't work backwards and forwards over an area to fill in gaps. To turn curves a gradual twist can be incorporated into the movement, but if the curve is too steep put the needle into the outside of the curve, stop and turn the work in the same way as for ordinary sewing. Corners can be worked in the same way as for normal sewing.

Machine settings

Stitch: Zigzag.
Length: Set on 0.
Width: Narrow to wide.
Thread: Experiment with a variety of machine embroidery threads.

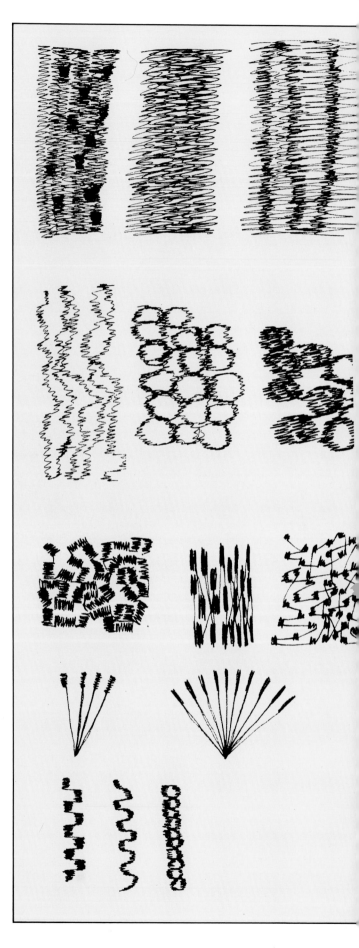

Stitch designs that can be created with free machine satin stitch.

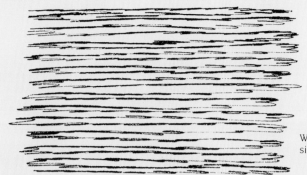

Work
sideways

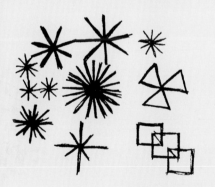

Carrying thread
goes to base of
next block

abcdefghijklmn

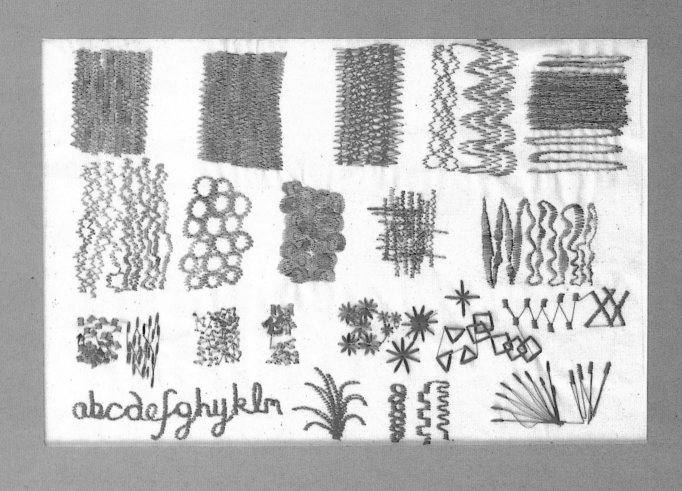

Sample of satin stitch from Experiment 5, worked on calico.

Experiment 5

- Work zigzag in vertical lines, towards and away from you. Work even and uneven stitch lengths. Work side by side and overlapping. Try including sections of satin stitch (closed zigzag) by slowing down the forwards or backwards movement. Try changing the stitch width – work a narrow width over a wider one.
- Work the same as above, but try making waves instead of straight lines. Variegated threads work well for satin stitch, or try a metallic thread to create a surface that could be interesting for further hand or machine work.
- Try working from side to side with the embroidery hoop. If you work very closely and carefully into the preceding stitch it is possible to create something that looks like split or stem stitching.
- Try some of the movements described for straight stitch. Weave stitch, working in circles, and even the 'drunken wiggle' can all look effective worked in zigzag or satin stitch.

- Try working rows of zigzag or satin stitch whilst changing the width control. This can be a little difficult – it would be a lot easier with three hands! – but the technique can be accomplished with practice. Try holding the ring with your left hand to the back of the machine and pulling it away from you, whilst changing the stitch width with your right hand. Your left arm should be resting on the bed of the machine. This technique looks better if the machine has an even rather than a stepped adjustment on the width control.
- Try working small blocks of satin stitch as beads. Experiment with the stitch width and the length of each bead. Work them in the same direction, or haphazardly

in different directions. (To do this the ring will have to be moved around as satin stitches can only be worked in line with the machine, from front to back, or back to front.)

- Use satin stitch blocks to apply small pieces of fabric.
- Use the blocks to move the eye and colour feel of a piece from one area to another.
- Use the blocks with straight stitch free embroidery techniques.
- Work satin stitch blocks to create a daisy-type flower design. Start with the machine at the widest stitch setting, then, keeping the hoop absolutely still, work between four and twelve stitches, finishing with the needle in at one side which will become the centre of the flower; turn the work carefully (always in the same direction – clockwise or anti-clockwise), being careful not to enlarge the central hole. Then work the same number of stitches again, finishing in the centre. Turn the work the same amount as before – imagine a five- and ten-minute segment of a clock face. Continue the process until the flower is finished. For variations, a second colour can be added using a narrower width stitch; or the stitch width can be altered as the flower is being made, giving the impression of a flower viewed from the side but be careful to re-centre after changing the stitch width. Your own experiments will yield a variety of daisy-type flowers.
- Work blocks using the thread in between the blocks to make part of the design. These threads between the blocks can normally be cut without the work becoming unravelled, but they can add to the design and texture of the work. Working with satin stitch blocks can be really effective when using a variegated thread.
- Try working a seed head (of the type shown in the diagram on page 38) by returning with a long stitch to a central point (use the hand wheel for this), then back to form another seed on the seed head. The block on the seed head can be worked with a narrow satin stitch (but work over the top part of the long stitch and then return to the central point); or use a wide zigzag worked horizontally in an exact line with the long stitch. Start and finish at the base of the seed, and work the stem by moving the fabric appropriately, and the hand wheel to make a stitch at the central point and then back to start the next seed head at its base always turning the hand wheel towards you; remember to swivel the ring so that the satin stitch is in line with the stem. The needle should be on the left when making the stitch at the base of the stem, and on the right when starting the seed head.
- Try working individual circles, varying the width of the stitch. Try open or closed zigzag. Try working a single circle, or imagine a spiral movement, but worked in a satin stitch.
- Alphabets and lettering can be worked in the same manner as straight-stitch lettering, but avoid as much as possible going over an area previously stitched, or work an open zigzag on the first pass, or a line followed by a satin stitch the second time. The effect is like writing with a scroll pen.

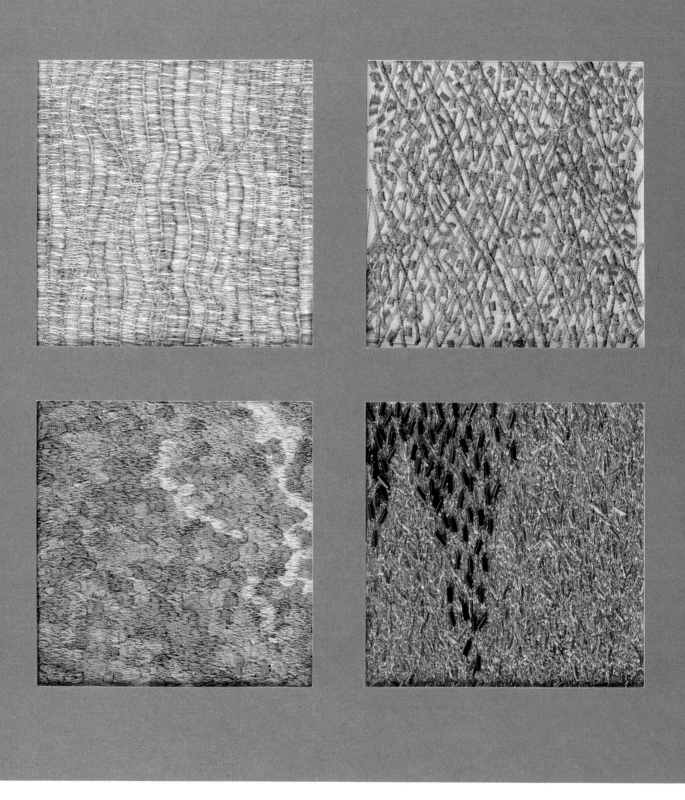

Samples of satin stitch from Project 11, based on an Autumn theme. Top left *Wide satin stitch in a variegated metallic in lines that are not quite straight. In between some of the rows there is fine satin stitch in gold.* Top right *A variegated thread creates a herringbone-type stitch with satin stitch blocks interspersed.* Bottom left *Circle movements with variegated and plain threads.* Bottom right *Wide satin stitch worked almost on the spot gives the long blocks which are interspersed with very small satin stitch blocks. Bugle beads were added by hand.*

Project 11

- Experiment with appliqué. Use free satin stitch for outlining the applied pieces; but also try free appliqué, where areas of fabric are bonded to a surface and the stitching is used for colour movement, but not exactly outlining each piece of fabric. You will find that even if a piece of fabric is completely bonded it will not stay in place well enough for washing and wearing, but by ensuring that each piece of fabric has some stitches in it everything can at least be held in place and re-ironed if necessary. If a lot of stitchery is to be included in the design, the applied pieces of fabric may simply be held down with small pieces of bonding fabric as this will make the stitching easier if the needle does not have to go through so many layers. If the thread wears too badly choose a larger needle or use a darning foot.
- Try mixing techniques of straight and zigzag stitching, working from drawings and designs, creating samples and 'notebook' pieces at first whilst you become more familiar with the techniques and marks and how they can be used together.
- Try working the techniques learnt with hand stitchery. Experiment and find uses for a mixture of favourite stitches. The following might be a starting point: bugle beads and bullion knots with satin stitch blocks; satin stitch daisies with 'lazy daisy', satin stitch as a padding for chain stitch; or try making straight or satin stitches that look like cross stitch, herringbone or cretan stitch, and mix with hand embroidery using the same stitch type.
- Encrust an area of machine work with beads, sequins or rich hand embroidery.
- Try working large-scale hand embroidery stitches and then machining into them.

Samples of free machine embroidery using automatic stitches. a) Worked in
greens using a 'leaf' motif which is variously lengthened and narrowed.
(Bernina.) b) Using a variety of stitches and a garden theme. (Pfaff.)

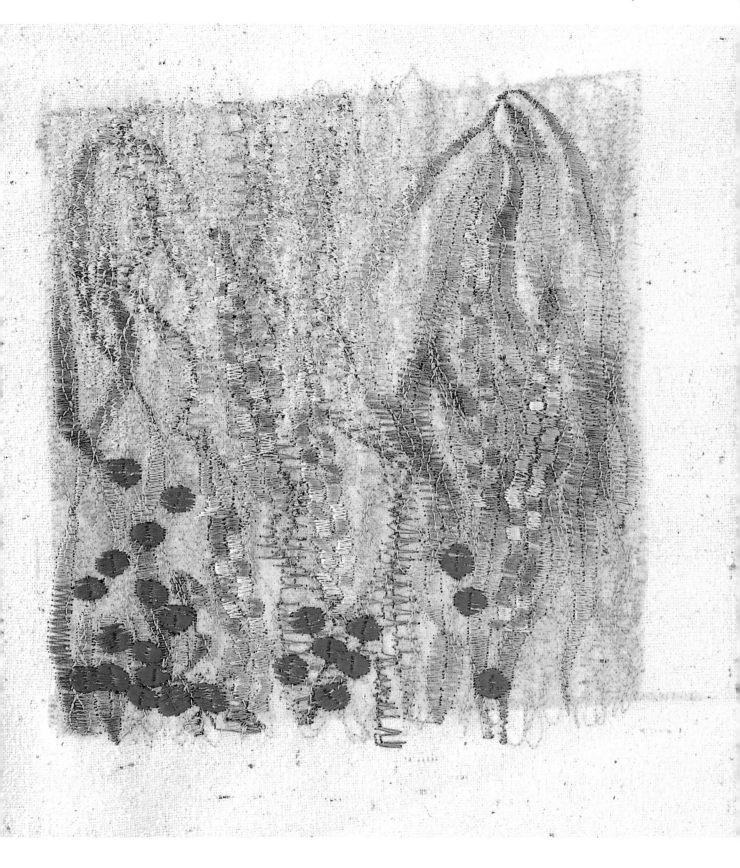

Working with automatic patterns

Automatic pattern stitches can become particularly interesting when worked with a free machining technique. The cams or computer will automatically guide the needle through the set stitch movements required for the pattern, and you simply have to control the hoop to create the stitch length. For this reason automatic patterns that rely on the fabric being moved backwards as well as forwards by the movement of the feed dog are unsuitable for this technique, as it will be impossible to judge when to move the fabric forwards and when to move it backwards if working freehand. Even so, the apparently haphazard needle movement that such stitches offer can be useful for textural areas – looking as they do a little like the 'drunken wiggle'. More suited to free machine embroidery are the automatic patterns that rely on the feed working only in one direction – any of these can be selected and changed with the width control, or elongated or mirrored if the machine has these facilities. The speed and direction in which the hoop is moved will now affect the appearance of the stitch, whilst the machine controls the widthwise position of the needle, so leaf shapes, wave stitch, scallops, shells – whatever patterns you wish – can be used.

Machine settings

Stitch: Automatic patterns.
Length: 0.
Width: The machine will select, but these can also be experimented with.
Thread: Machine embroidery.
Tension: Normal – but the top tension may have to be loosened to achieve a good result with zigzag stitches.
Foot: No foot, but lower the lever!
Feed: Lowered or covered.
Needle: 80.
Fabric: In embroidery hoop.

Project 12

- Experiment with the automatic stitches that are available, to see what sort of finishes can be created.
- Try mixing these textures and patterns with other methods of free stitching to create interesting surfaces and images.

Experiment with the techniques described in this chapter as well as those in chapter 2 to come to your own conclusions about when to use the darning foot. Although the darning foot has specific uses as described, how much it is used for other types of free embroidery is a matter of personal choice and how worried you feel about stitching your fingers. It is most unlikely, however, that the needle will go into your fingers as long as you concentrate and always look at what you are doing!

Machine embroidery offers many opportunities for texture and colour mixing. Experiment and practice will help you to realize the possibilities and create your own original ideas.

Most important, do not become lazy about changing the threads. Frequent colour changes – between plain and plain or plain and variegated shades – will improve the look of an embroidery. Changing the thread from a shiny to a matt one in the same colour can also be effective. Working as I do on a lot of embroidered gardens, as well as architectural and figurative images, I need a lot of colours. For example, to ensure that I can always use exactly the colour I want, I have built up a collection of over one hundred green shades alone. And I use all of them! Try to collect as many machine embroidery threads as you can – you will never have enough colours.

Mother and child *Worked mainly in straight stitch on a silk noile ground with outlines worked in a variegated silver thread. The wallpaper background is worked freely with two different colours in a twin needle and a narrow zigzag. (Bernina.)*

4

Tension Techniques

I have met embroiderers who assume that it is essential to adjust lower tensions in order to work successful free machine embroidery, automatically employing a loosened bobbin case whenever working without a foot! From the preceding chapter you will have noted that successful machine embroidery can be created using a 'correct' tension, and further adjustments are not necessary. However, working with tension techniques can add another dimension to machine embroidery. More colours can be added more quickly by using a different colour through the needle to that on the bobbin, with both appearing on the surface of the embroidery. A wide variety of textures and patterns, beyond those already discussed, can also be achieved.

Changing tensions on the machine should not be a worry. Machines are designed with tension screws that can be adjusted without causing damage (the notion that it will is a myth), and reference to chapter 1 will help you to reset the correct tension after you have finished working with changed tensions. The top tension on the machine will be governed by a wheel that is either numbered or has a plus and minus symbol. To increase the top tension turn the wheel towards a higher number or the plus sign. The bobbin tension on a vertical bobbin race will be adjusted by a screw (see page 10). When loosening this screw by turning anti-clockwise, always do it over fabric stretched in a ring, as it is very small and easily lost if loosened too far. If it should pop out it will then drop onto the fabric, and thus be easily found. On a horizontal race machine there will also be a screw to adjust tension – the one to use will usually be facing upwards. This screw often has numbers and a location mark so that it is easy to reset. If it does not have numbers make a note of the angle of the screw before you start to adjust it, so that it can be reset easily.

It is tempting to make copious records of how certain effects are achieved when adjusting tensions. This can be difficult when using a machine with a vertical bobbin race, although the position of the screw can be described in terms of the hands of a clock. In practice I find that such notes are unnecessary. If you are thoroughly aware that you are trying to pull the bobbin thread through to the top of the fabric by varying degrees to create a variety of effects, the nature of the adjustments necessary to create more or less bobbin thread on the surface of the fabric will be self-evident. A tighter top tension will pull through more bobbin thread, a loose bobbin tension will allow more thread to be pulled through.

If the machine has a vertical race it is often easier, although not essential, to have a spare bobbin case which can be used for tension techniques. On page 10 there is a description of how to reset a vertical bobbin case. This shows that having only one case need not cause any problems. However, occasionally screws can wear and tend to move when the machine is running fast, so to avoid this happening (a very rare occurrence) on normal sewing, and for convenience, it may be preferable to have a bobbin case which is always ready for normal sewing. The spare bobbin case to be used for tension work should be marked in some way (some manufacturers supply spare bobbin cases that are marked); otherwise use nail varnish or paint to indicate which is the 'tension' bobbin case. It is a good idea to reset the screw after it has been used on different tensions, so that you know how it is set next time you come to use it; alternatively, keep it set on a favourite setting in between use.

An important point to remember when adjusting tensions is the notion of 'give and take'. If one tension is tightened to 'take' (i.e. to pull the other thread through to that side of the fabric), but the other not loosened to 'give', the technique will work, but the thread 'taking' will be more likely to snap, particularly if the machine is run fast. If the thread that is to 'give' is set on a looser tension, then the thread 'taking' will be able to do so more easily. If both threads should be set loose in error, both will be 'giving' and none 'taking' and the loose threads may snap as they get caught in the bobbin race.

Whip, cording and feather stitches

Whip stitch refers to a machine setting where the top thread is pulling the bobbin thread through to appear on the surface of the fabric. Both the top thread and the bobbin thread will show. The bobbin thread will feature in anything from small dots to small loops.

Cording is where a medium whip stitch is set using the tension adjustments, but the top thread is completely covered with the bobbin thread by making the stitches very close together; staying on one spot can cause interesting bobbles to occur, although do be aware that this can cause the top thread to wear and break more easily. Cording can be achieved using machine embroidery threads, or thicker top threads can be used which have the advantage of 'automatically' tightening the top tension because of their relative thickness in relation to the gap between the

Some patterns are more suitable than others for whip and feather stitch.
Try patterns based on those illustrated here.

Samples of whip stitch, feather stitch and cording using straight stitch and zigzag. All the work is free machine stitching apart from the bands of automatic stitches bottom right.

tension wheels. With thick threads some tension adjustment may also be required (though less than normal) and a thicker needle of 90–110 will be necessary, for example, a number 12 pearl cotton requires a 100 or 110 needle.

Feather stitch is a stitch where big loops occur on the surface of the fabric because of a very loose bobbin tension, and through the use of a tight or very tight top tension. The patterns used with this stitch can be important as straight lines can give an unstable stitch and glue will have to be used on the back to prevent the loss of the stitches. If curves or circles are used the stability of the stitch is increased.

These stitches are the most common forms of tension techniques and are achieved by bringing the bobbin thread through to the top of the work – slightly for whip stitch, more so for feather stitch. In order to bring the bobbin thread to the surface of the fabric the top tension can simply be tightened (many modern machines will work quite happily with the tension tightened as far as it will go). The top thread may have a tendency to break, but by choosing a cotton rather than a rayon this will improve. Many effects can be achieved by this method alone, and if the work is done fairly slowly the top thread will not break too often. If, however, the bobbin tension is loosened as well, it will be seen that more bobbin thread is pulled through to the surface of the fabric, the top tension can be

adjusted so that it is tight (but not over-tight) and thus the thread breaks less often. Working quickly can create a different amount of pulling to a slow speed, so try this on your machine.

Machine settings

Stitch: Straight and zigzag.
Length: Set on 0.
Width: As desired.
Thread: Experiment with a variety of machine embroidery threads, including a transparent thread for the top of the machine.
Tension: Experiment as suggested.
Foot: No foot; lower or cover the feed dog. Remember to lower the foot lever to engage top tension.
Needle: 80.
Fabric: In a hoop.
Note: When loosening the bobbin tension the top should always be at least a little tight; if both threads are loose they may get caught underneath and break. If you are

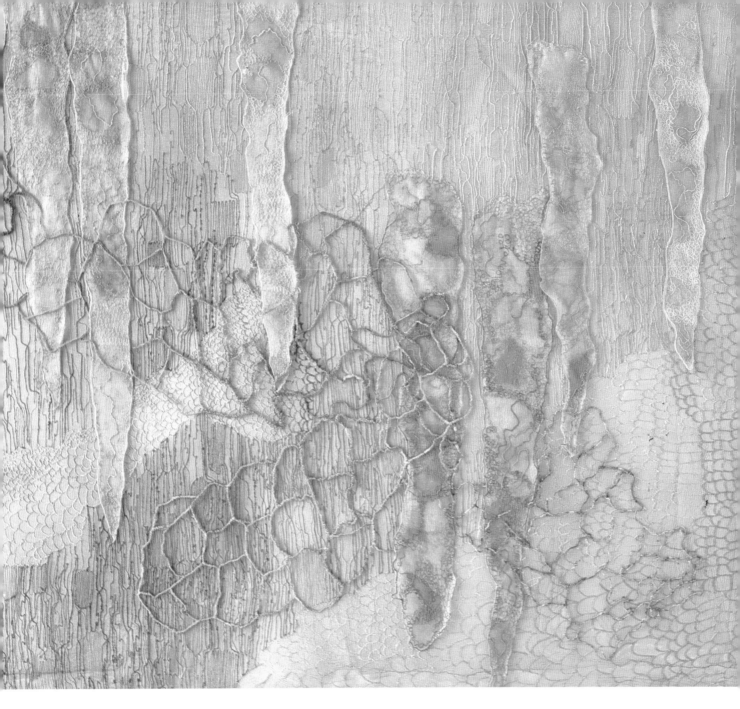

working on a horizontal bobbin race machine you can bypass the tension for the more extreme effects by putting the bobbin into place, but not pulling the thread through the cut-out in the bobbin case but simply threading it through the hole. Bypassing works easily on a horizontal race machine, but as it is not necessary, or often not possible, on vertical race machines similar effects are best created by loosening the tension screw.

On vertical bobbin race cases with a large cut-out section, i.e. Pfaff, the bobbin tension can be bypassed easily and the result will be a loose feather stitch.

Experiment 6

- Work in straight lines, curves, circles and vermicelli stitch. Gradually tighten the top tension until it is as tight as it will go without constantly snapping – use a

An embroidery inspired by stonework worked in whip stitch and cording on dyed silk. The free hanging pieces are edged with a firm corded stitch (see chapter 5). (Worked on an Elna by Roma Edge.)

machine embroidery cotton number 50 or 30 as this will be stronger than rayon.
- With the tension thus set, try working with stitches very close together (imagine the stitch length used in satin stitch) to create a corded or wrapped appearance. Adjust the top tension until the top thread is neatly and tightly covered by the bottom thread.
- Try working with longer stitches to make dots of colour further apart. By using a different colour top and bottom the colour on the surface of the embroidery can be varied according to how frequently the stitches are

made, as each stitch will create a 'dot' of colour from the bobbin. The top tension can also be turned up and down to create changes in colour – when the tension is high more of the bobbin thread will show, and if it is turned low the top thread will be the only colour visible.

- Experiment with satin and zigzag stitches to see how they behave with a changed tension.
- Working with the foot in place, the feed up and no ring (i.e. for normal sewing), experiment with the automatic stitches available on your sewing machine.
- Now try loosening the bobbin tension by a small amount – the top tension can be adjusted down a little.
- Experiment with stitches as above, gradually adjusting the tensions until you are working with the tightest possible top tension and the loosest bottom tension, and try bypassing the bobbin tension if this is possible on your machine – see machine settings on page 51.
- Now experiment with the different tensions with the variety of stitch patterns and movements suggested in chapter 3.

Project 13

- Working with cording and whip stitches, try making a design worked in rows of straight or wavy stitches; include areas of circles or vermicelli. This could be worked on dyed or layered fabrics, or try working on quilted fabric with a darning foot – the fabric could be put in a ring for ease of movement. Change both the needle and bobbin thread frequently or use variegated threads. Try metallic threads in the bobbin.
- Try working feather stitch. Experiment with wiggles, curves, spirals and circles.
- Mix feather stitch, cording and whip stitch with ordinary free machine embroidery techniques. Try adding wrapped cord, satin stitch beads and anything else you might think of to create a rich and textured surface.
- Try working in monochrome or in one variegated thread.
- Try working with many colours – a colour scheme may be chosen by placing a selection of bobbins together to find something that appeals, or find a painting or printed piece of fabric and copy the colour scheme from that, being careful to use the colours in the correct quantities.
- Metallic threads can add richness to a finish, so experiment with these. Use a number 90 needle (except for the smooth fine metallics which will work with a number 80). These threads work best with a looser top tension, so compromise by using a top tension that is only just tight and a loose bobbin tension; alternatively, use them on the bobbin and bring them through to the surface with a tight top tension and a loose bottom tension.

  Metallics could also be used in ordinary machine embroidery techniques to add richness to surfaces stitched with tension techniques.

Using thicker threads for machine embroidery

Machine embroidery threads are available in an extensive range of finishes, and can be all that is needed to create a wide variety of textures. However, the rougher metallic threads and some hand stitch yarns can be used through the needle of the machine. Simply increase the needle size until the thread can pass comfortably through the eye and the needle pass up and down through the fabric without the thread wearing or becoming jammed underneath. Always work slowly at first and listen to the machine, so that if it jams, or sounds unusual, you can stop immediately and put right any faults, removing any scraps of thread which may be left in the bobbin race. You can then try again – check the basics: tension correct, foot lever down – and if necessary use a larger needle as this will help. If the machine continues to jam, reset it for normal stitching with a machine thread, then try again. If the machine jams, continued attempts at stitching can cause the bobbin race to become misaligned – so always stop immediately!

Most of the rougher metallic threads intended for machine use work happily with a 90 or 100 needle, although the top tension may need to be lowered, and a slower machine speed (or at least an even machine speed) is best. Other threads which can be used include buttonhole twist, quilting thread, number 12 pearl cotton (use a 100 needle) and even number 8 pearl cotton with a 120 or 140 needle – try a machine specialist for these. These thicker threads have the effect of 'automatically' increasing the top tension as they work through the small gap in the tension rings – and this, plus their added strength for increased top tension, is something that can be used. They also provide more bulk for wrapping when using corded whip stitch.

Using such threads on the top can thus offer a new textural interest, but even thicker hand stitch threads can be used on the bobbin.

Cable stitch

Cable stitch is the name given to the technique where a thick thread is wound onto the bobbin and the work is done in reverse. The bobbin thread remains on the underside of the fabric, and will, when the work is finished, form the right side of the embroidery.

Many threads can be used for this method so experiment with whatever is available. A good general rule is that the thread should not be furry or fluffy as this will catch in the bobbin race. Try some of the following: stranded rayon, soft embroidery cotton, pearl cottons numbers 8, 5, and 3, other rayon threads, 1.5mm ribbons, knitting cottons, cords and silk threads.

Threads can be wound onto the bobbin by hand if they are not on a spool If you are using cottons, cords and a machine with a horizontal bobbin race then the tension can be bypassed (see *Machine settings*, page 51); the result cannot be controlled, but it is usually very acceptable. When using a machine with a vertical race the screw on the tension spring will have to be loosened to allow the thicker thread to pass through the sprung metal clip, but so that the tension is still tight (thus the tension has been loosened, and yet there is still a *tight* bobbin tension). The top tension can be kept at 5 or adjusted towards minus. Further adjustments of the top tension will change the effect on the reverse side from cording or couching to a whip or feather stitch. Cording or couching are the easiest to work in the first instance as you can be sure of exactly where the thicker thread is being held because it is exactly in line with the stitches on the needle side of the fabric. (With whip and feather stitch this will not be the case so leave these until you have had a little practice.) Lowering the bobbin tension further to give a looser bobbin tension on the thread will make the thicker thread 'bobble' more and so create more texture – but the top thread may break with this method if it is too loose, so watch the tension settings carefully!

When working with thicker threads the bobbin tension screw may be loosened considerably, and if it is very loose the action of the machine can cause it to become looser still. Very occasionally, it is possible for the screw to spring out whilst working. The change in the machine sound will tell you that this has happened, and if it does do not try to continue stitching. The machine will not be damaged, and the bobbin case can be put back together and sewing recommenced. But just in case this should happen, when sewing with a loosened bobbin tension, particularly with thicker threads, it is vitally important that the cover or door on the bobbin assembly should be kept closed so that if the bobbin case should spring apart all of the pieces, including the tiny screw, can be found inside the machine bobbin race area rather than on the floor!

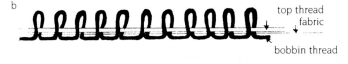

Thread tensions. a) Whip stitch: the bobbin thread loops over the top thread in small loops; cording is worked with a similar tension, but the top thread is completely covered by using small stitches. b) Feather stitch: the bobbin thread creates large loops on the surface of the fabric. c) Cable stitch: the top thread makes small loops around the thick bobbin thread, couching it into place.

The effect created by cable stitching is similar to that achieved when setting up a whipped or corded stitch to appear on the top side of the fabric, only in reverse. The top thread will couch or cord (according to the length of stitches that are made) the thicker thread into place on the underside of the fabric. Go slowly at first, so that any problems can be identified. If the bobbin tension is not

loose enough, or the thread is too fluffy and has caught, the machine may make stitches but it will be difficult to move the fabric as the thread underneath will not be running. Rethread if necessary, loosening the bobbin screw a little more to allow the thread to be pulled through more easily (or perhaps the cause is too much thread on the bobbin and it is getting caught). Maintain a tight bobbin tension, i.e. the bobbin case would not drop if held and tapped (see chapter 1). Fairly thick threads can be used for this method, but the thicker they are the easier it should be to flatten them so they can pan through the tension spring – thus a thicker silk than cotton can be used, and a fine ribbon will pass through because it is flat.

On a horizontal race machine, the bobbin tension will have to be bypassed; on a vertical race machine this can only be done on an 'open' bobbin case, eg Pfaff, but anything that is likely to work will work with the bobbin tension in operation and the tension spring loosened – with the added advantage that you are in control. The maximum thicknesses of thread that can be used is about the same on both although slightly rougher threads can be used on a bypassed tension. The bobbin case on a Pfaff machine is, however, designed differently to other vertical-race machines, and works excellently with a bypassed tension.

With a carefully set tension, no problems should occur, and it will be found that stitching with this technique can give quick covering results, a highly textured surface, in some ways similar to some hand stitch techniques, and areas can be worked and worked over again almost as easily as with normal machine embroidery. With very thick threads it will be found that the bobbin will hold very little, but a number of bobbins can be prepared in advance if a large project is envisaged.

Machine settings

Stich: Straight or zigzag.
Stitch length: Set on 0.
Width: As desired.
Thread: For the first experiment use different thicknesses through the needle, thereafter machine embroidery threads on the top, different thicknesses of thread and hand stitch threads on the bobbin.
Tension: Experiment as suggested.
Foot: No foot, lower or cover feed dog, lower foot lever to engage tension.
Needle: Up to 140 for first experiment, thereafter no 80.
Fabric: In a hoop.
Note: To hand wind the bobbin, hold the thread against the rim of the bobbin, wind a few times to secure the thread then cut off the loose end to prevent it catching in the tension spring. Continue winding but do not overfill as it will make smooth running more difficult.

Experiment 7

- Try a variety of threads on the top of the machine, and see how they can be used to enhance the tension techniques so far discussed.
- Experiment with a variety of threads on the bobbin. Try

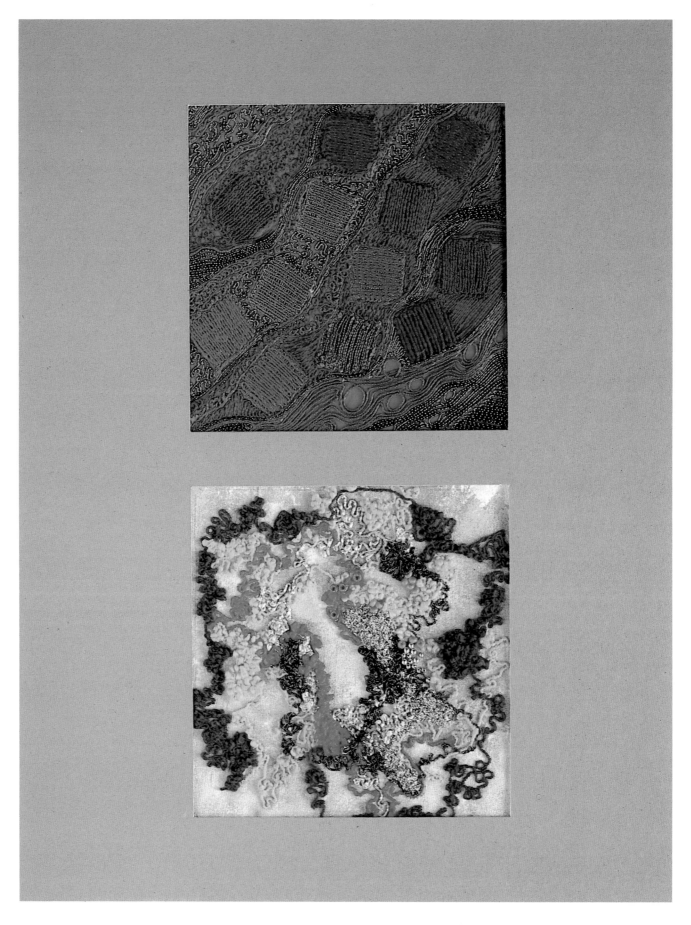

using contrasting or self-colours for the top thread, or use a transparent thread.

- Try adjustments on the bobbin tension between tight and loose (if possible with the thickness of thread being used). Remember the rules of 'give and take', so keep the top tension normal or a little tight if a loose bobbin tension is used.
- Return the bobbin tension to tight, and experiment with the top tension. Normal or just loose will couch the bobbin thread (or cord over it if stitches are close together); loosen the top tension further and feather stitch will be created on the underside. A tight bottom tension, with or without a thicker thread, using a normal top tension, will make 'bubbles' in the fabric surface (top side) when circles are drawn.
- Try working with zigzag and satin stitches. To create a satin stitch on the underside with a thicker thread, a more open zigzag appearance will be required in the normal machine embroidery thread which is being employed on the top of the machine.
- With the foot on, the feed dog up and no ring, try experiments with bands of automatic stitches.

Project 14

- Try using cable stitch techniques for a linear embroidery – use lines, vermicelli stitch and circles with a couched or corded line.
- Try creating a solid stitched appearance with cable stitch. Experiment with the different textures that you have discovered.
- Using cable stitch heavily, fabrics can be manipulated and warped – try stitching in circles, curves, backwards and forwards to create different movements in the fabric. Try working on different fabrics, including felt.
- Try mixing cable stitch with other embroidery techniques, use machine and/or hand embroidery, beadwork, etc. Draw on the wrong side of the fabric, remembering to reverse the image, or machine enough of the image

from the right hand side to act as a guideline when working the cable stitch from the wrong side. If you change the bobbin thread whenever you change the top thread in any ordinary machine embroidery on a piece of work that is to receive cable stitching, it will be easier to recognize where to do the cable stitching.

- Cable stitch works well when couched or corded, so work a design based on closed lines of different colours. Try couching with a gold thread to give a reverse *or nué* effect, or add other types of stitching to enhance the texture.
- If soft threads are used, the machine can work repeatedly over the same area (try working backwards and forwards in one direction, then at right angles to this). Repeated quantities of thread can be added until the top thread wears and breaks. Experiment with creating encrusted surfaces, mixed with other textural techniques, or bead and goldwork. Additional textures could be added with vanishing lace techniques, which will be discussed in chapter 6.

Working with a machine, confidently changing and resetting tensions, learning to hold a ring and operate it to create numerous patterns, controlling the machine speed for intricate effects, or having the confidence to work fast when it is simply a matter of 'filling in' – these are all skills that can be acquired with practice.

Having attained a level of confidence and competence with the machine, there are many areas of pure machine embroidery that can be enjoyed. But besides creating patterns or pictures on areas of fabric, there are many other techniques which can offer avenues of exploration to the embroiderer. Many techniques are related to hand embroidery, others can only be worked on the machine. The machine will be seen as a tool that not only makes interesting surface stitchery but can also be used to create fabrics and laces, edges and holes, as well as three-dimensional objects. In the remaining chapters I aim to explore these techniques and offer some inspiration for their use.

Examples of cable stitching. Top A tightly tensioned bobbin results in a smooth couched thread. The squares are worked over in two directions and applied to the felt ground. A variety of medium-thickness hand embroidery threads are used; the top thread is a self colour in most cases. Threads used include oiska yarn, perle cotton, soft embroidery cotton and rayon à broder (Bernina). Bottom On a sponge-dyed silk ground this cable stitching is done with a loose tension through bypassing the bobbin tension completely. Threads include soft silk (unspun), oiska rayon, metallic hand stitch thread, rayon à broder; the bright pink and light blue are hand knitting ribbons. (Pfaff Creative Machine 1473.)

An embroidery inspired by the gardens at Barnsley House in
Gloucestershire. The knot garden pattern is taken from one in the garden,
the colour scheme is inspired by the laburnum and wisteria arch which is
underplanted with violet allium. The knot was worked with a straight stitch
(bricked) from the right side of the fabric. The fabric was then reversed for
the cable stitching. Worked on a silk ground.

5

Insertions, Openwork and Edges

These related techniques rely on the secure binding of an edge to create their result. They can be used on their own or if used with other methods of embroidery they will add interest to a piece of work by providing a change of depth. Thus they can be employed on panels and hangings, but are especially useful for interior decor and garments.

Each method and embroidery technique featured in this chapter does have a traditional application and design and these are often useful as starting points when practising the techniques; it will be seen that design ideas can go a lot further through adequate 'paperwork' or worksheets, or through repeated sampling.

Inspiration for enhancing the techniques will be gained by working them as provided in the projects section. But first it is necessary to identify the various techniques and learn how to adapt them to machine embroidery.

Reverse appliqué

First a chosen piece of material, larger than required, is pinned or tacked behind the main fabric, then the shape required is stitched with a straight stitch (twice on the same line for firmness). This can be done with free machine embroidery or with the foot and feed in place, according to the intricacy of the design. Having worked the straight stitch the top fabric can be cut away from the inside of the stitched shape up to the stitching line. This is best done by separating the two fabrics by rubbing them between thumb and forefinger, snipping the separated top fabric, and cutting out to any awkward corners. The fabric can then be folded back towards the stitching line, and snipped away neatly. The edge can be neatly finished off with a fine satin stitch – the needle should enter just into the reverse appliqué fabric, and into the main fabric side of the two lines of stitching. Other automatic patterns could be used instead of satin stitch, or free machine embroidery might be appropriate. Any remaining applied fabric on the reverse side can be trimmed fairly closely, or up to this stitching if the reverse side is likely to show.

This technique can also be used to create a type of 'mola' work, where a number of layers of coloured fabric are put together. The first lines of machine stitching are worked, then the layers cut through to reveal the desired colour, and the final neatening stitching worked over the edges.

Shadow work

This is created as for reverse appliqué, but by placing coloured fabrics under a see-through fabric surface. The stitching is worked to apply the fabric shape, but the area cut away is the unwanted section of coloured fabric, external to the lines of machine stitching on the reverse side. The appliqué can be finished off with satin stitching if required. Other ideas could include trapping pieces of coloured fabric, beads, sequins, paper, etc, between two layers of see-through fabric with haphazard machine stitching.

Simple insertions

A piece of lace, see-through fabric, or machine-made vanishing fabric lace (see next chapter) can be inserted into a fabric using the same method as reverse appliqué.

Openwork

Simple openwork

Working in an embroidery hoop to hold the cutwork shape open, the same method can be used as for reverse appliqué. Stitch the desired shape with two rows of straight stitching, one on top of the other. Keep the shape simple – i.e. square, circular, oval, or hexagonal, not star-shaped or with many curves. Cut out the shape to the line of the stitching, and work a satin stitch over the edge to finish it off neatly. The needle should go into the hole and then into the fabric on the other side of the stitching, thus completely covering the straight stitching and binding the edge. (Look at the notes in chapter 3 to see how best to create a satin stitch with free machine embroidery.)If you are working a circular hole, it may help to bring in the first two fingers of the left hand (for a clockwise motion). These fingers can be placed each side of the circle to help in the swivel movement of the work, producing a curve. The other hand remains in place on the hoop to provide stability. Remember that when stitching a curve it may be necessary frequently to adjust the position of the hoop, a manoeuvre it may not be possible to carry out smoothly, so whenever it becomes necessary stop with the needle in the fabric on the outside of the curve and move the hoop as much as is required before continuing stitching.

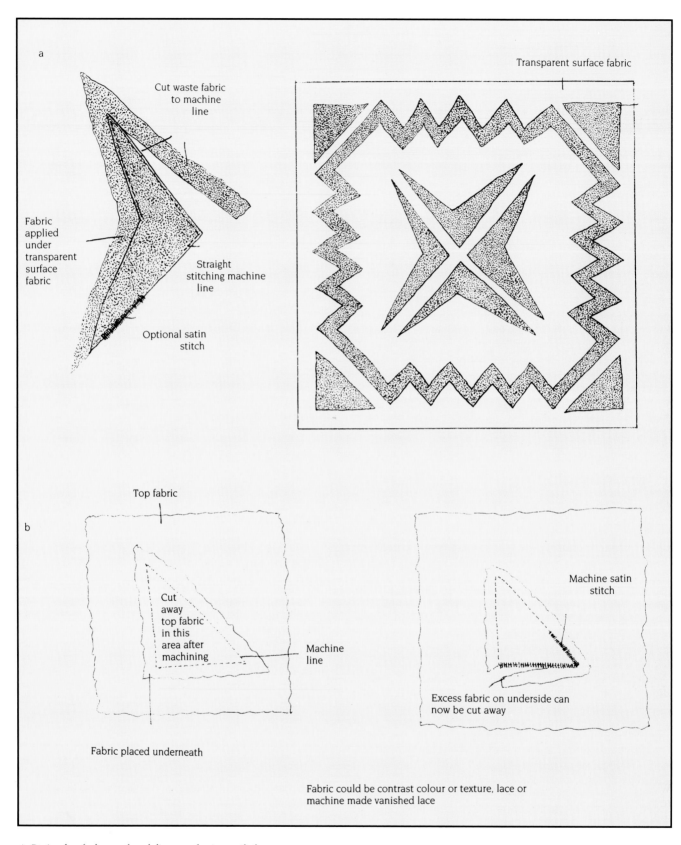

a

Cut waste fabric
to machine
line

Transparent surface fabric

Fabric
applied
under
transparent
surface
fabric

Straight
stitching machine
line

Optional satin
stitch

b

Top fabric

Cut
away
top fabric
in this
area after
machining

Machine
line

Machine satin
stitch

Fabric placed underneath

Excess fabric on underside can
now be cut away

Fabric could be contrast colour or texture, lace or
machine made vanished lace

a) Design for shadow work and diagram showing method.
b) Method for reverse appliqué or simple insertion. Cutting away the excess
fabric on the underside is optional, and need only be done if it is likely to
show. Shadow work relies on a transparent top fabric, reverse appliqué can
be done with any top fabric.

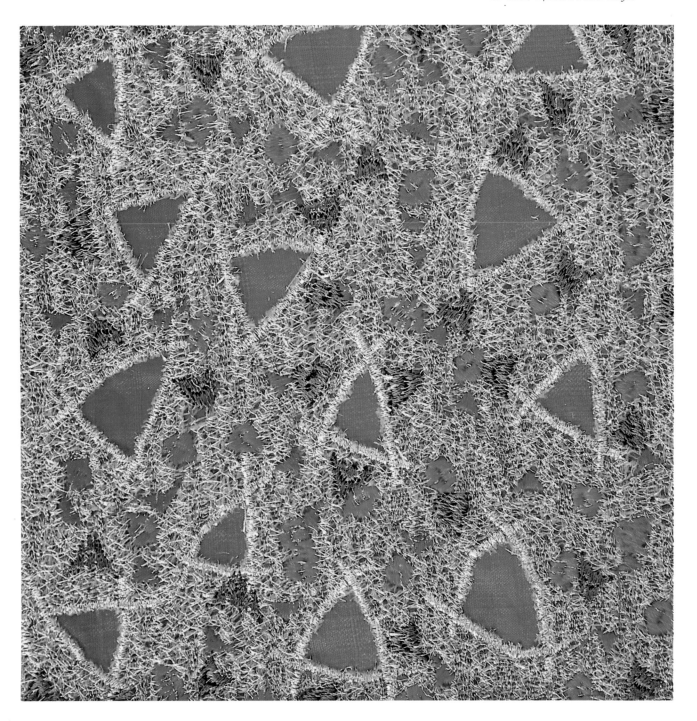

Openwork with stitched fillings

With the fabric in a hoop, stitch the required shape in two rows, then cut out the centre. Working with small stitches, and fairly slowly (free machine embroidery – no foot or feed), stitch across the fabric hole. Do not move too fast or the fabric may give way at the edges. A line can be drawn backwards and forwards two or three times; more lines can be added in other directions, or parallel to the first. They may be satin stitched to neaten them if required. Finally the edge of the fabric hole can be bound with a satin stitch.

Scrim worked with pulled work in a gold thread (see chapter 7) is applied to a fabric and more stitching is added. Areas of triangles are delineated by three satin-stitched lines and the top scrim fabric is cut away to reveal the coloured silk beneath.

Making lace textures in a fabric hole

Work two rows of stitching and cut out the required hole. Work backwards and forwards over the hole, then again at right angles; further stitching can also be added as required. When the lace is finished it can be cut from the hole and applied to other embroideries for additional textural interest. This method should be worked without foot or feed with the work in a hoop.

Eyelets

Eyelets can be worked as for simple openwork, and this method does mean that you are in complete control of the size of the eyelet and hole. However, an eyelet attachment is available for most machines. It usually comprises a cover plate for the feed with a point for the location of the eyelet hole, or a larger hole into which other attachments with varying sizes of locating spikes can be fitted to give larger and smaller eyelet holes. Awls may also be supplied to make the eyelet, and a special foot to fit the cover plate. With these attachments eyelets are easy, if a little predictable.

Put the work in a small hoop, make a suitable size of hole in the fabric and place it over the locating spike. Then check the needle position and stitch width, and sew continuously and evenly while turning the ring to create an even eyelet. Fixing instructions are always provided with these accessories, so attaching them to the machine should not be a problem. Larger eyelets can be made – if a little untidily – by pulling the fabric against the spike as the stitching is worked.

Shisha work

Shisha work is an Indian technique, worked by hand, which incorporates pieces of mineral glass or mirrors onto an embroidered fabric using lace work and a buttonhole stitch. It is possible to create a similar effect by machine. Simply make eyelets of an appropriate size (i.e. slightly smaller then the glass so that it can be trapped), then make a sandwich out of the fabric with the eyelets, the shisha glass underneath the holes, and another layer of fabric underneath. (It may be easier to glue the shisha to the backing fabric before making the sandwich.) A running stitch or a machine-stitched line around the outside of the glass will hold it in place under the eyelet hole. Working from the reverse, perhaps using a cable stitch, will help. If a slightly transparent backing fabric is used the edges of the glass can be seen and thus avoided when stitching. Cable stitch will give a more ethnic, handworked quality to the work.

Buttonholes

Most modern machines have an automatic or semi-automatic buttonhole. These can be used to create a change in depth of surface. Try working them, then slashing them and placing them onto other fabrics. The holes may be stitched, tied together, or laced through.

1 *a) A typical eyelet attachment. b) Method of holding and turning hoop when working with an eyelet attachment; a smaller hoop is best. c) Many eyelet attachments can create a variety of different-sized eyelets.*
2 *a) The types of shapes that can be made when creating holes or eyelets with free machining. b) Straight stitch first, then cut hole, then satin stitch. c) Method for carrying threads across the hole, worked before the final satin stitch. d), e) and f) Further ideas for carrying threads which can be cut out and removed to be used to add texture to another embroidery, as g).*
3 *Method for simple cutwork or reverse appliqué where the satin stitch is worked first and the fabric trimmed to the stitching – the edge will not be as neat as method 2.*
4 *a) A design for shisha work. b) First work eyelets in a top fabric. c) The shisha glass is sandwiched between the eyelet fabric and a base fabric with an encircling stitch.*

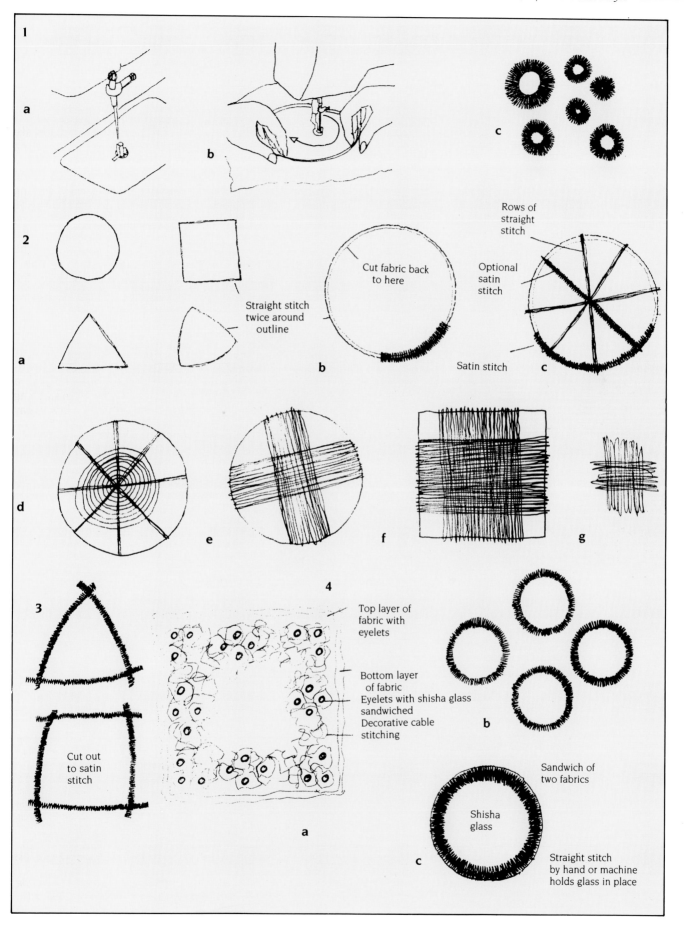

1

a

b

c

2

a

Straight stitch twice around outline

Cut fabric back to here

b

Rows of straight stitch

Optional satin stitch

Satin stitch

c

d

e

f

g

3

Cut out to satin stitch

4

Top layer of fabric with eyelets

Bottom layer of fabric
Eyelets with shisha glass sandwiched
Decorative cable stitching

a

b

Sandwich of two fabrics

Shisha glass

Straight stitch by hand or machine holds glass in place

c

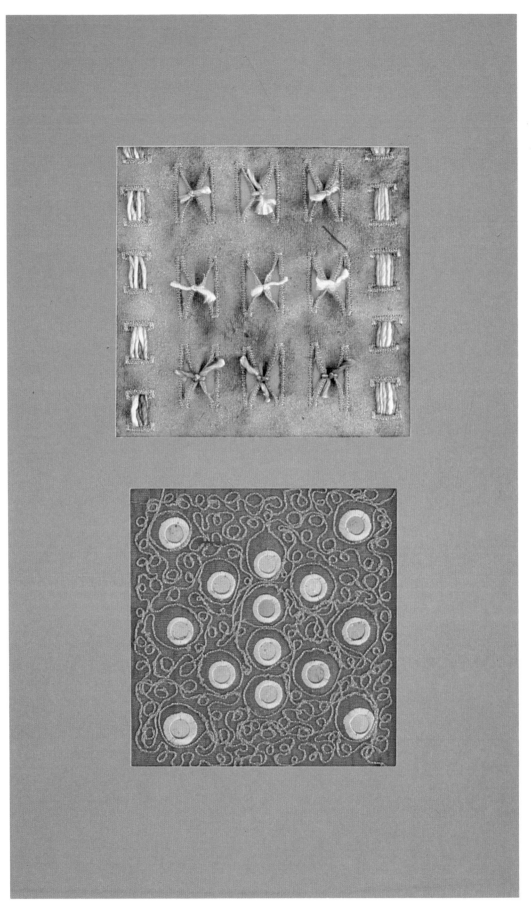

Top Worked on a sponge-dyed noile silk ground. Automatic buttonholes are tied together or laced through with soft embroidery silk. This rich surface could be used for a Renaissance-style sleeve or jacket. Bottom Eyelets worked on a silk ground with shisha glass sandwiched with a cable stitch, couched with a gold top thread for added richness. The shisha is lightly glued to the backing to hold it in place. The cable stitch, worked from the reverse side, enables the glass to be seen whilst machining so that it can be avoided.

Top A grid of straight
stitches was stitched onto a
sponge-dyed silk ground,
and alternate squares were
cut out. The edges were then
stitched with a satin stitch
following the same grid lines.
Bottom Worked on
sponge-dyed noile silk, freely
worked eyelets, some with
carrying threads, using a
variegated metallic thread.
Gold stitching was added to
the background to increase
the richness.

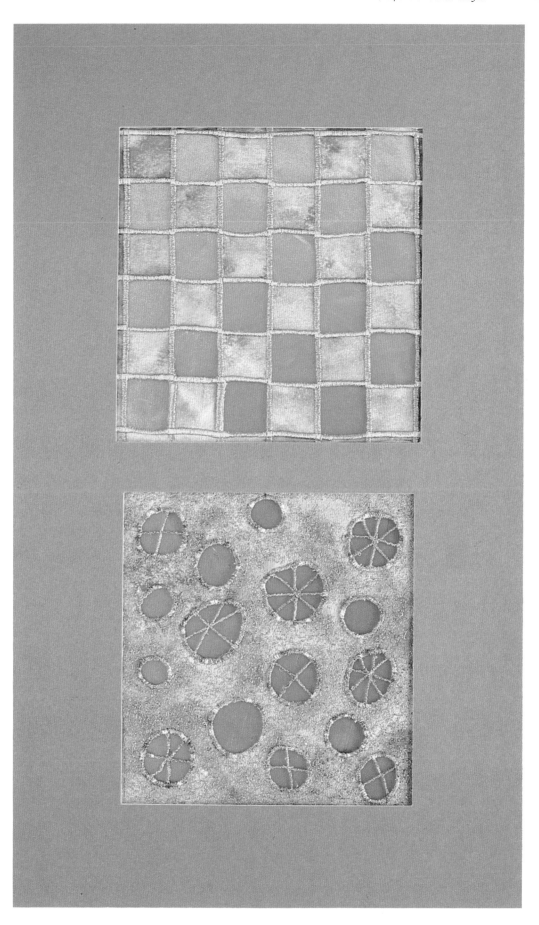

Insertions

Simple insertion stitches

These are usually automatic stitches that can be used to create traditional insertion or faggoting stitches between two pieces of fabric to act as a seam. Check your machine's handbook for individual recommendations.

Two pieces of fabric, each with turned edges, are placed under a foot (usually a grooved foot). The stitch selected should enter each of the pieces of fabric at its extremes, leaving a gap in the centre. Insertion stitches of this type can also be achieved using a tailor's tacking foot and the fabrics prepared as before. Use a loose top tension, and start and finish with two or three stitches on one spot. Zigzag or satin stitch over the bar on the foot. When the fabric is removed from the machine and pulled apart, it will be joined by insertion stitches.

Insertion stitches with vanishing fabric

Using cold or hot water vanishing fabric (see the next chapter for information on which would be best to choose), tack two pieces of fabric to each side of a strip of vanishing fabric. Formal or informal designs can be used. The edges of the fabric can be turned in or not, according to the needs of the design (the fabric need not have straight edges if this is not appropriate). The fabric can be machined to the vanishing fabric, not tacked, if the machine lines are going to be covered by the design.

For a simple formal piece, straight stitch along the edge of the fabric applying it to the vanishing fabric – the edges can be turned under for added neatness. The insertion stitches can then be worked across the vanishing fabric, as you would do for stitched fillings on openwork. Ensure that all stitching works into the fabric side of the holding stitching before working back across the vanishing fabric. It is important that all satin stitching across the vanishing fabric is worked on top of a number of rows of straight stitching, otherwise it will fall apart when the fabric is dissolved. When the insertion stitches are complete, the first row of straight stitching along the edge of the fabrics can be stitched over with a satin stitch which should be worked with a zigzag into the vanishing fabric and then into the fabric side of the stitching. Thus the edges of the stitching and fabric will be neatened.

A freer design can be worked by turning the edges of the fabric in and tacking them to the vanishing fabric. (These tacking lines can be removed when the stitching is finished.) The stitching can now be worked haphazardly over these edges in a loose design and onto the main body of the fabric, as well as across the vanishing fabric to form the lacy insertion. If the edges of the fabric were to be cut and satin stitched, an even looser design could emerge through not having to use straight edges. The uncut fabric should be stitched to the vanishing fabric along the lines which are to be cut on both sides of the insertion. The fabric can then be cut away to this stitching line, the insertion stitching completed, and the edge of the fabric finally satin stitched as described above. Alternatively, if there is enough free machine embroidery over the edges,

satin stitch may not be necessary. When the work is completed the vanishing fabric can be dissolved (see next chapter).

Machine settings

Stitch length and width: As desired for technique.
Threads: Machine embroidery.
Foot: Appropriate for technique.
Needle: 80, ballpoint if using cold water vanishing fabric.

The machine may be used with or without feed and foot – choose which ever is appropriate for the design.

Experiment 8

Experiment with all the techniques so far described in this chapter until you are familiar with how to achieve a good result.

Project 15

- Try a design worked on two layers of different coloured fabric. Work eyelets and enclose shisha glass, include areas of reverse appliqué to the second fabric. Simple insertion pieces could also be added for a further dimension. Attempt to create a rich and ethnic look, or perhaps the design could come from ideas based on water – the sea, waterfalls, etc.
- Consider reverse appliqué with more than one layer to cut through to create mola work.
- Shadow work could also incorporate areas of cutwork or eyelet embroidery.
- Experiment with different sizes and shapes of holes when creating lace in space. Use different stitching patterns. These samples could be added to other experiments to create a more intense texture. Try using variegated threads in the needle, and a metallic thread on the bobbin (or vice versa). Or the stitching could be in white with a yellow spiral centre to give the impression of a daisy for three-dimensional work.
- Eyelets could be threaded with thick threads or ribbons in an organized or a haphazard manner.
- Work eyelets into a fabric which can then be sponge- or spray-dyed; try working on felt for added texture.
- Incorporate eyelet holes with shisha, or try placing large sequins or pieces of paper or foil, or previously stitched fabric behind the eyelet holes.
- Eyelets could be worked evenly and then used for gathering or smocking.
- Try eyelets on quilted or very fine fabrics (the former to be worked without an eyelet attachment).

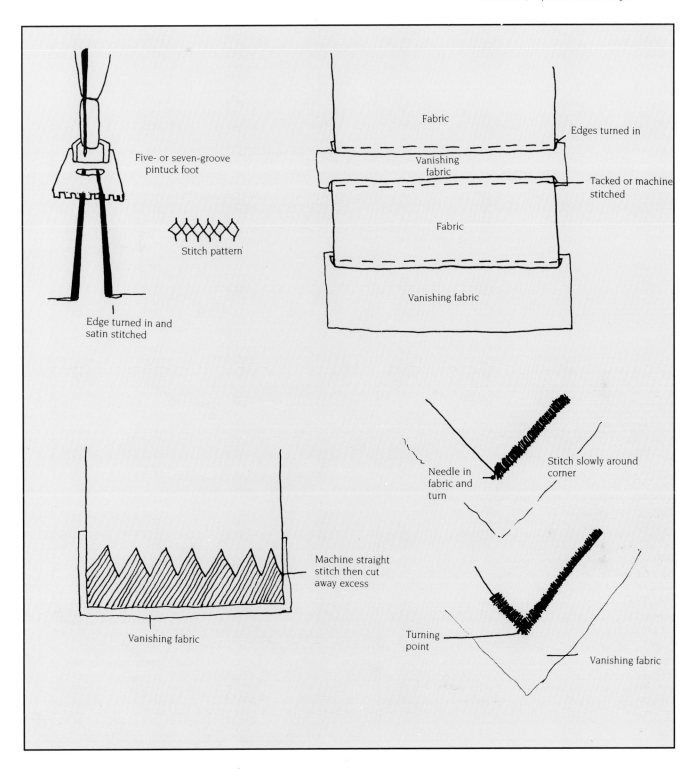

Five- or seven-groove
pintuck foot

Stitch pattern

Edge turned in and
satin stitched

Fabric

Edges turned in

Vanishing
fabric

Tacked or machine
stitched

Fabric

Vanishing fabric

Machine straight
stitch then cut
away excess

Vanishing fabric

Needle in
fabric and
turn

Stitch slowly around
corner

Turning
point

Vanishing fabric

a) Working a fine formal insertion. b) How fabric and vanishing fabric are
put together for free insertions. c) Fabric attached to vanishing fabric for an
edge that would otherwise be difficult to work. d) The points of the fabric
can then be easily stitched over to provide a firm edge.

Worksheet of ideas for free insertions and edges worked on fabric with vanishing fabric.

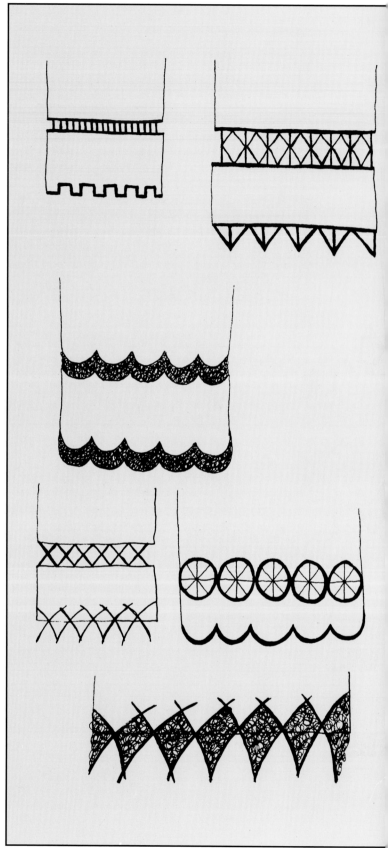

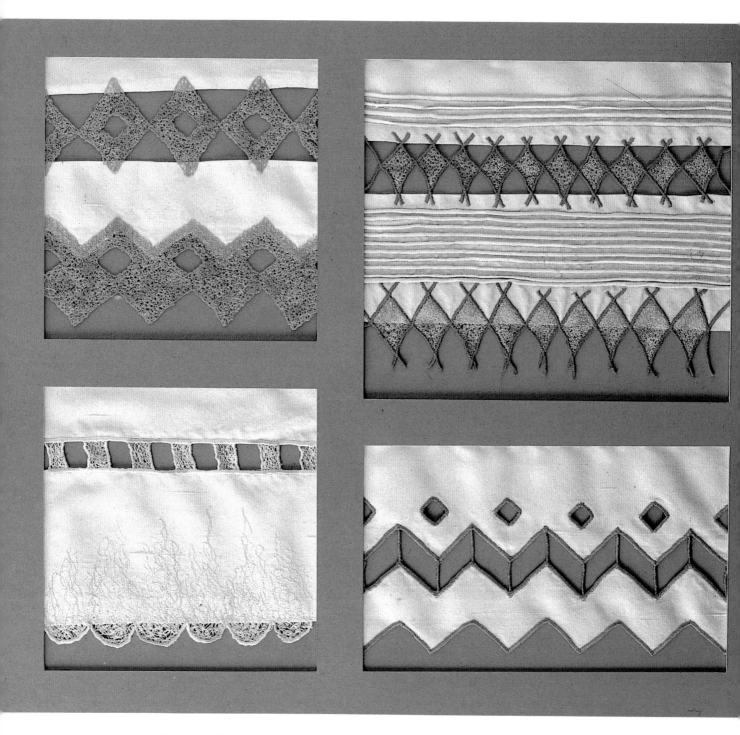

Examples of insertions and edges worked on silk and using hot water vanishing fabric. All stitching, apart from the example bottom right, was done freely; the piece bottom right used a foot and feed.

- Experiment with buttonholes. Threads and ribbons could be laced through them. They could be stitched open or tied to enlarge the hole, or to reveal a fabric underneath. This technique could work well to create full sleeves with a Renaissance richness – so try working on panne velvet or satin.
- Buttonholes or eyelets could be threaded with cords, or cords and tassels could emerge from them.
- Experiment with insertion stitches. Create a formal appearance. Traditional drawn thread work may provide inspiration. Try working bars by machining straight lines and then satin stitching over them. These bars could be further manipulated by hand, using drawn thread methods.
- Experiment with informal insertion stitch designs. The joined pieces of fabric could be cut in shapes to work with the lace stitching on the design. Organic designs, wrought iron work or art nouveau designs may offer sources of inspiration.

1

2

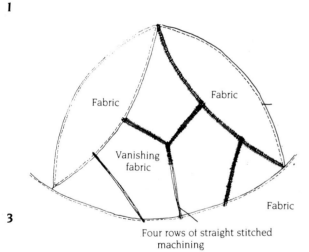

3

Four rows of straight stitched machining

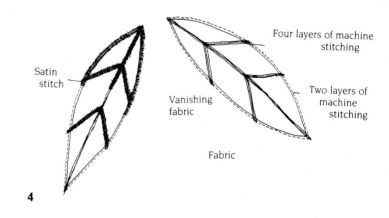

4

- Insertion stitching could be matched by an edge worked over vanishing fabric.
- Experiment with insertions in openwork and into other holes cut and filled with a vanishing fabric which can be stitched and dissolved. Such areas may work well co-ordinated with other types of insertion work or simple cutwork.

Cutwork

This traditional hand embroidery technique can be tedious and time-consuming. It is much quicker to work the technique by machine, although it still requires patience and a great deal of care and attention to detail.

The following explanation and diagrams describe how to work a traditional cutwork design. The method can of course be adapted to a more contemporary approach which could include layering see-through fabrics, or creating an appliqué or dyed surface before starting cutwork.

1 *The formal cutwork design—black areas indicate fabric to be removed.*
2 *Design with lines in cut-out areas to show stitched bars. 3. Close-up showing an order of work to avoid too many thread ends. 4. The working of the leaf shapes in the fabric.*

Using machine-embroidered lace worked on vanishing areas, an even more open piece could be created. Such embroideries would work well in one colour, or in soft harmonies of pastel shades. Rich reds, blacks and golds would lend sumptuousness to these techniques. Follow the instructions below for basic cutwork:

1 Trace the design onto the material using your favourite method. For this technique the design could be traced onto architect's quality tracing paper, which can be placed on the fabric. Use a machine line with very small stitches to trace all necessary lines onto the fabric, except those that are to be satin stitched bars. The tracing paper can then be removed along the perforations. Tracing paper is better than tissue for this method as it is more easily removed.

69

2 The fabric should now have all the edges which are finally going to be sewed and satin stitched; do not include the joining bars. Stitch them again, but first place a piece of hot or cold water vanishing fabric behind the design. Hot water vanishing fabric is best for this method as it will withstand any amount of satin stitching – unfortunately, the cold water fabric would be likely to perforate and tear.

Although it is possible to add the vanishing fabric after the areas of fabric have been cut, it is better to stitch it into place first as it will hold more open areas of cutwork in place.

3 Cut away all unwanted areas of fabric back to the two lines of stitching. Be careful not to cut through the vanishing fabric, which should be left intact. Should any vanishing fabric be snipped by mistake it can be repaired by tacking in another piece.

4 Straight stitch any bars between areas of fabric – this should be done up to four times to create a good base for the satin stitch that is to follow.

5 Satin stitch over the straight-stitched bars. When doing this try to formulate an order whereby each end of each bar will be stitched over when another bar is worked, until the only ends that have not been stitched over are those that finish on the fabric. The satin stitch should only be worked to the edge of the fabric (vanishing fabric side), otherwise it will add bulk to the final satin stitch which is used to neaten the edges.

6 Finally satin stitch around the fabric edges, making sure that each edge is bound and all stitching onto the fabric is neatened. Again, stitch over as many 'starts' and 'finishes' as possible to avoid too many thread ends – these can be cut off once stitched over.

7 Any thread ends remaining will have to be threaded through to the back of the work and finished off with a knot to prevent unravelling.

8 The work can now be immersed in water (see next chapter) to dissolve the vanishing fabric.

It is important that you continue working through to this stage. The work will look much better once the vanishing fabric is removed, as the satin stitch tightens up on the edge and looks neater. This technique is quickest worked in a hoop with free machine embroidery – and will make you an expert on free-machined satin stitch! But if absolutely necessary it can be worked with a foot on, although this is more time-consuming. If you are not skilled enough at free-machine satin stitch, work the straight stitches with the fabric held freely in a hoop, then put the foot on for satin stitch and work normally.

Edges

Satin stitch edges

It is possible to satin stitch a piece of fabric where the desired edge is to be, and then cut back to the satin stitch using sharp scissors. This does, however, give a slightly 'frayed' result. A better appearance will result if the desired edge is straight stitched first, the fabric then cut back to the stitching, and the satin stitch worked over the edge. A further, wider row of satin stitch can be added if desired.

This method can be worked on paper, or 'stitch and tear' along the edge for a firmer and more easily achieved result. Work with the foot on and the feed dog up.

Corded edges

Cords may be attached to a previously satin stitched edge; binding in a cord with another satin stitch or blind hemming stitch will add more firmness. Work by oversewing a previously satin stitched edge and at the same time guide through a pearl thread, taking care that it is not stitched into place under or over the edge. To sew a corner, drop the feed control, sew three stitches, leave the needle in the work at the inside edge, raise foot, turn work, make a loop with the cord, lower foot, sew three stitches, raise feed, and continue stitching carefully. Pull on the loop until the foot no longer lies on the corner. To make the loop disappear, pull on the end of the cord. Push corner stitch over corner and continue stitching.

Edges on stretch fabrics

Working over a cut edge with a satin stitch on the cross of a fabric whilst pulling the cross grain, or working on a stretch fabric that is stretched as it is sewn will create a wavy edge.

Turned satin stitch edges

This produces a firm edge, suitable for many applications including garments and soft furnishings, and can make a useful decorative bound edge as an alternative to a facing. Turn the excess of the fabric under to the required edge and pin or press into place, then stitch over the edge with a satin stitch to secure. The waste fabric on the reverse side can now be trimmed back to the satin stitch, leaving a reasonably tidy edge on the wrong side as well. Work with the foot on and feed up.

When working with these methods it will probably be necessary to hold the threads to the back of the machine when starting off (even if this is not normally necessary on your machine) and pull them a little for the first few stitches until the feed dog has a hold.

Cut and sew

Some machine manufacturers make an elaborate foot which comprises a small pair of scissors which move as the needle goes up and down – the machine then satin stitches over the newly cut edge which is held exactly in the right position. Instructions for using the foot will be supplied with it. It is an expensive accessory so consider carefully whether you will do enough of this kind of work to warrant such an investment.

Edges with automatic stitches

Most modern machines have a range of stitches which will produce a satin stitched scalloped edge, or a blind hemming stitch which can be used to make a scallop over the edge of a soft fabric such as jersey – work on an edge that has been turned in. The blind hemming stitch can also

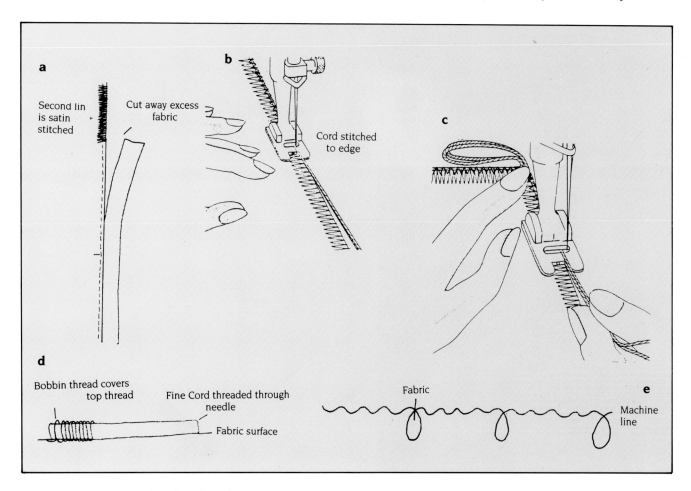

a) *A simple edge.* b) *Applying a cord to a satin stitched edge.* c) *Working a corner on a corded edge; the end of the cord is then pulled to get rid of the loop.* d) *Diagram of creating a whipped cording over a thicker thread.* e) *Freer edges and designs can be worked with a whipped cording; the excess fabric is cut away after stitching.*

be used to attach a cord to the edge. The 'creative' section of your machine handbook will deal with these techniques, which can be useful, if a little pedestrian.

Edges with whip stitch cording

An effective edge on fine fabrics can be created by using free machine embroidery with a corded line. Refer to chapter 4, on tension techniques, and put a number 12 pearl cotton or buttonhole twist on the top of the machine, with a machine embroidery thread of the desired colour finish on the bobbin. The top tension must be just tight enough (or loosen the bobbin tension as necessary) to bring up the bobbin thread until it is wrapping the thicker top thread evenly, and without loops. Use a larger needle (100). Work the stitches close together so that only the bobbin thread is visible, but it is important that the work stays on the move to avoid bobbles of thread; also, if the needle should work into the same stitches, it is likely that the top thread will break. Because the work is done freehand in a hoop it is possible to stitch intricate shapes and curves. When the work is complete the waste fabric can be cut away. This edge is quite firm but will not stand up to rough wear and tear.

Edges on small pieces of fabric

All the edges so far discussed have assumed that the fabric is a comfortable size to handle under the foot or in a hoop,

but sometimes (sewing leaves or petals, for example) this may not be possible. In such cases the piece to be worked can be stitched with a straight line onto 'stitch and tear' or vanishing fabric – the latter is probably the most suitable as the 'right' and 'wrong' side will look the same. Vanishing fabric may also be dissolved to a point where it leaves a residue in the fabric, and the resulting work can be dried into a desired shape that will be held firm by this residue. If you are working on vanishing fabric it is probably best to put the work in a hoop. For 'stitch and tear' this will not be necessary.

Having secured the piece of fabric to the vanishing fabric or 'stitch and tear' the edge can now be satin stitched to secure it against fraying – work the satin stitches into the item and then into the holding fabric. The 'stitch and tear' is torn away after use, and the vanishing fabric will be vanished afterwards (see next chapter).

Another alternative for edging small pieces of fabric is to bond two pieces together (different colours can thus be used). The shape can then be cut out, and the edge stitched with a satin stitch using a normal foot and the feed dog engaged. Hold the threads when starting and pull a little to

Cushion worked from a hand cutwork design on a linen ground. (Worked
by Gloria Jenkins on a Pfaff machine.)

help the work through the machine. Be careful that any pulling is even. This method helps when pieces are just large enough to handle; the firmness given by the two layers and the bonding fabric helps to prevent the work from being dragged down into the base of the machine.

Machine settings

As appropriate according to the technique.

Experiment 9

- Try all the techniques listed and keep records and samples of the results.

Project 16

- Try a creative approach to cutwork – using the techniques described in this chapter – with dyeing, layering and any other machine embroidery techniques that may seem appropriate for a richer finish.
- Experiment with different edges on different fabrics and incorporate your findings with other methods such as insertions or openwork.

Examples of edges worked on a Cornelli machine. These could also be worked using the corded method described. (Worked by Tania Cuthbert whilst a student at Manchester Polytechnic.)

6
Lacy Effects with Vanishing Fabrics

In about 1879 the first attempts at 'chemical' lace were made on a continuous thread or schiffli machine. Paper was used as a background for the embroidery, and designs were made which would hold together when the paper was washed away. This process presented two problems: small pieces of paper would remain in the work even though the embroidery was thoroughly rubbed; and the paper did not form a solid enough ground for the embroidery, breaking into pieces and causing irregularities in the stitching.

This came to the attention of Charles Wetter who was determined that something better could be achieved. His first attempts were made with a muslin that could be dissolved away after stitching, but then, through a happy accident, he became aware that silk dissolved in a chlorine solution. If the embroidery were worked in cotton, this, being vegetable based, would not dissolve. It took some time to perfect the techniques necessary to stop the delicate lace structure falling apart when the silk backing was dissolved, and the chlorine solution proved injurious to health. The first problem was solved by using lace workers to teach the embroiderers some of their interlocking stitching techniques, the second by substituting caustic soda for the chlorine solution, and so the process was patented. From 1885 'chemical' lace was made on the schiffli and hand machines.

At first, copies of popular laces were produced, but eventually individual styles emerged which did not resemble anything handmade and these became known as 'guipure' lace.

Between 1885 and 1895 a 'chemical' lace was developed working in silk on a nitrated cotton base which could be dissolved in a blast of hot air in a special furnace; but the first chemical method remained the most popular.

The invention of rayon acetate reduced the cost of 'guipure' lace as work could now be done with cotton threads on a cheaper ground which was then dissolved in acetone. This method is still in use today, but to the domestic embroiderer it presents a number of problems: pure rayon acetate is increasingly difficult to find, as well as being expensive; and the use of acetone as a dissolving fluid is smelly and unpleasant, particularly if working on large-scale pieces.

Vanishing muslin, a chemically treated cotton fibre which dissolves when dry heated, was the first fabric to be really useful to embroiderers outside industry, and was heavily in use in colleges by the end of the 1970s. Hot water vanishing fabric, which is a pale blue-green closely woven fabric resembling organza, reached the shops by the mid 1980s, followed shortly by cold water vanishing fabric which resembles a fine transparent plastic. These last three are the most useful, easy and cheap to use for the domestic embroiderer. Between them they offer enough versatility for any design. Each has its own peculiarities which makes it ideal for certain applications and less useful for others, and for this reason I will deal with each of them separately.

Vanishing muslin

This brittle fabric can be used either held very carefully in a hoop, or used with a foot on the machine. If using a darning foot move slowly with a faster machine speed to prevent puckering and tearing. If using a ring, a bound one would be best, and try to get the fabric taut first time; if the sides are tugged to increase the tautness, the fabric will tear. Straight lines and grids are fine for this fabric, but if working in circles, choose a loose, even tension and work with small stitches to develop a ground that will hold the fabric together. Rows of satin stitch (which must be done over rows of straight stitching in order to hold together) are a problem if you are using an iron to destroy the fabric as they prevent heat reaching the fibres. Any threads can be used on vanishing fabric as most survive when heated (surprisingly), but white thread is perhaps the most vulnerable as any discolouring is more obvious.

To vanish the fabric use a hot iron, and if possible a metallic ironing board cover to increase the heat. The iron is kept on one or two adjoining areas continuously until the muslin goes brown, and then moved onto the next area. The muslin can then be removed by rubbing the work between your hands. Do not be alarmed – if the work is well designed it will hold together! The work can be rubbed in this manner until all or most of the blackened bits of muslin are removed, and any remaining pieces will have to be picked out with a needle.

An alternative method is to place the work on a baking sheet or foil in a preheated moderate oven (350°F, 180°C, gas mark 5), for 5–6 minutes. The threads are unaffected by the heat and stay in better shape than after being ironed; again the work will need a little rubbing between the fingers to remove the last traces of muslin.

The advantages of using vanishing muslin are that any thread can be used, although be careful in the choice of any added fabrics, as they will have to withstand a hot iron. The fabric itself can be selectively vanished, leaving areas of muslin which can be dyed or used to add texture to a design.

Vanishing muslin does have a 'shelf life', so buy from a supplier where they have a reasonably rapid turnover, and only buy in quantities you are likely to use. The exact 'shelf life' is difficult to determine, as one can never be sure how old a fabric was when it was acquired. But the effect of age on vanishing fabric is that it becomes more difficult to vanish, and eventually will not vanish at all – I know to my cost that this last stage happens at around five years old!

Cold water vanishing fabric

Cold water vanishing fabric is fragile and will stretch easily. It is best used in an embroidery hoop. Place the fabric on top of the larger ring and smooth out. Put the smaller ring into place. If there are any puckers, repeat the process. The screw can be fairly tight so that the fabric will hold once it is in the ring with just a small amount of tightening.

Because the work is vanishing in cold water any thread or fabric can be used that will stand cold water. Designing, however, requires some attention – heavily worked areas of straight stitch can cause the fabric to disintegrate, and satin stitch can perforate the fabric so badly that it will fall apart, so more open textures are better. If an area is going to be filled in solidly, make a gridwork first on which to do this.

A loose, even tension is best for this fabric, and a ballpoint needle is essential to avoid tearing. But using it double, as sometimes suggested, is not necessary if these precautions are taken.

To vanish the fabric, cut off any excess then put the finished work under running cold water, although warm water works even better. If the work is simply placed in a bath of cold water and agitated, the fabric will disappear leaving a residue that will stiffen the embroidery, which can then be moulded if desired; running warm water will remove all of the residue; so any desired finish can be achieved.

Cold water vanishing fabric is the cheapest material and the quickest and easiest to vanish. It can be as easy to sew on as muslin providing care is taken in design, but its nature can still make it difficult to work on, and some sewing machines flatly refuse! But perseverance with this fabric is rewarded.

Hot water vanishing fabric

This fabric not only looks like organza, but also works like it. It can be placed in an embroidery hoop and tugged tight like any fabric. Any design can be stitched onto it, and the hoop can be moved around easily and as often as necessary. Any needle can be used, although a ballpoint is best. Any threads and fabrics can be used and attached to it, bearing in mind the limiting factor of the vanishing process.

This fabric is so quick and easy to work on that, of course, there has to be a drawback, and this is that it only vanishes in hot water or, rather, to be completely vanished, boiling or lightly simmering water. To do this most successfully, bring a large amount of water to the boil in a saucepan and simmer the work (having cut off any excess fabric) for 1–2 minutes. With larger pieces the water 'exhausts' so it is necessary to repeat this process two or three times with clean water until all the residue is removed. As with cold water vanishing fabric, the process can be halted at any time to leave a residue in the fabric to stiffen the embroidery.

Some fabrics and threads will not withstand this process, but test fabrics before dismissing them as unsuitable because the results can be surprising (even a silk chiffon may withstand boiling!). Most importantly, metallic threads will not withstand boiling, becoming crumpled, hard and misshapen (perhaps this could be useful for more unusual embroideries!). Metallic threads can be incorporated into a design that is to be boiled up to about 10–30 per cent, otherwise try one of the following methods:

1 Place the work into as large a shallow dish as possible to fit into a microwave oven, and immerse in water. Bring the water to just under simmering point and choose a low power to keep the water at this temperature. Watch the work carefully, and at the first sign of crumpling take it out. This process can be repeated with clean water.
2 Place the work in a large flat dish and pour successive kettles of boiling water onto it until the fabric has dissolved.

It will be noticed that even with cotton threads the work will shrivel when placed in the boiling water. This need not be a cause for alarm, but work done on hot water vanishing fabric will have to be stretched back to the original shape and size after vanishing and may even need to be pinned to a board to dry. This is not necessary with either of the other fabrics. Do not iron the work before it is dry as this seems to stiffen it. For large pieces that are to hang evenly it may be prudent to use only one type of thread so that any shrinkage will be even and more easily stretched flat.

Being fully aware of the capabilities and drawbacks of each fabric should mean that you can make the best decisions about which fabric is most suitable for which design. At first I found cold water vanishing fabric slow and difficult to use, but I have now conquered its peculiarities. Thus I tend almost entirely to use this and hot water vanishing fabric as they are so much easier to vanish.

Stitch and pattern design for independent lace structures

It is essential to remember that when the fabric has been vanished the threads will be all that is holding the created fabric together. For this reason the lace structure must interlock and there are many stitch and pattern designs that will do this. Although an elaborate interlocking overall design can be made on these fabrics, it can be dangerous to try an elaborate design at a first attempt because one which looks as if it will hold together will often prove disappointing when the fabric is vanished. Begin by trying a selection of patterns and grids that a design can be added to, or by varying the colours in the stitch pattern worked,

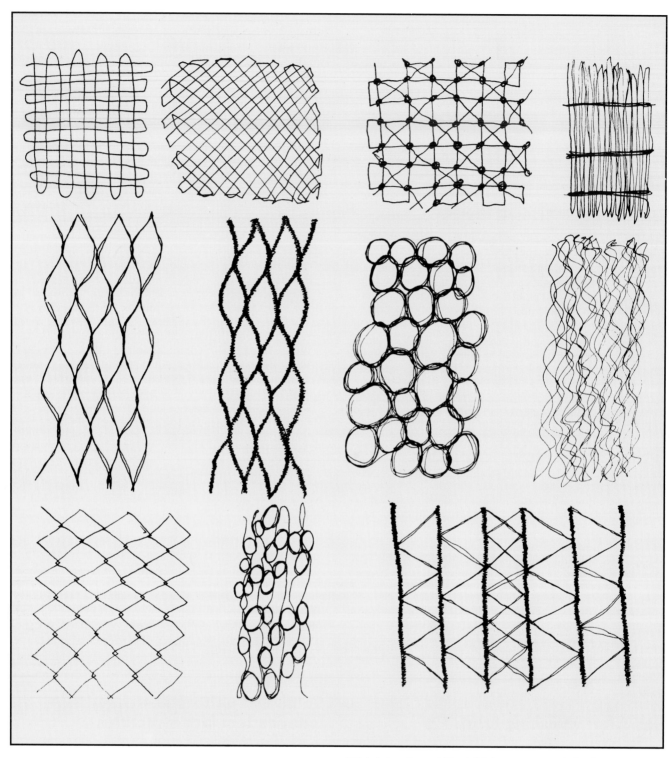

Stitch designs for vanishing fabric lace structures which will hold themselves without being attached to a surface.

through which the design can be incorporated.

Whenever a design relies on threads touching, make sure that they don't simply touch as they might with normal machine embroidery, but that one thread actually just passes over the other to form an interlocking stitch; thus the design will be held together. Any minor errors can be repaired by hand; major disintegrations can either be discarded, placed on more vanishing fabric and reworked, or included on other embroidery and have more work added to provide a textural effect.

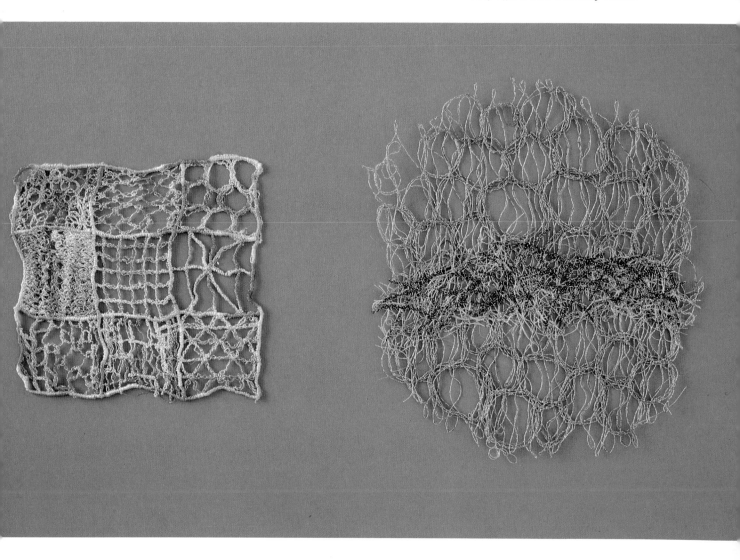

Samples of lace. Left Worked on hot water vanishing fabric with a variegated thread using a variety of stitch patterns. Right Worked on cold water vanishing fabric with metallic threads in wave stitch, circles and crosses.

Machine settings

Stitch: As appropriate.

Length: Use a short length to prevent puckering. If working freehand achieve this with a fast machine speed, but move the hoop slowly. On cold water vanishing fabric use a medium-length stitch.

Width: As appropriate.

Fabric: In a hoop for any free machine embroidery, although vanishing muslin will work with no hoop and a darning foot.

Thread: Machine embroidery; experiment with a variety.

Tension: Normal.

Needle: Fine, 80. Use a ballpoint on water-dissolvable fabrics.

Note: The introductory remarks on each of the fabrics will help to establish which are the best methods and designs of stitchery for each fabric.

For the most part there is little advantage in working with tension techniques. It must be borne in mind that it is the position of the fabric between a tight and loose thread that makes the loops which make loose whip stitch and feather stitch interesting. If this fabric is removed the copious amounts of loose thread involved will make a disorganized and unclear design. A fine whip stitch and cable stitching will work. Satin stitch must be done over rows of straight stitching as it is only a closed zigzag and with the fabric removed it will open out into a straight line.

A 'gimp' thread is a thicker thread used to pick out shape and stabilize a lace design.

Experiment 10

Work each of the following on each type of vanishing fabric to ascertain which is best, or use whichever you think most likely to be successful:

● Make a simple grid. Use an ordinary foot and straight stitch, or stitch freehand with the work in a hoop.
● Work a trellis-like grid, as above.
● Work a grid over and over three or four times then satin stitch over the result. Work freehand or with a foot.

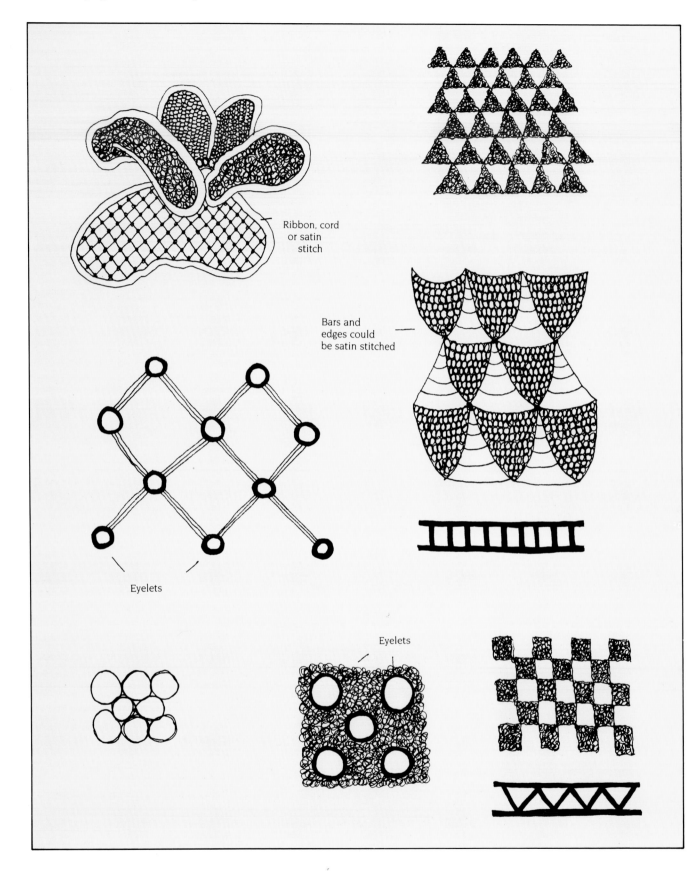

Ribbon, cord
or satin
stitch

Bars and
edges could
be satin stitched

Eyelets

Eyelets

Worksheet of ideas for independent lace structures taken from handmade
lace techniques. Eyelets are worked over circles of straight stitch to prevent
the satin stitch disintegrating.

- Work a trellis grid over and over three or four times, then satin stitch on the lines.
- Work overlapping circles.
- Work re-emphasized circles or squares, ensuring that the lines interlock.
- Work rows of vertical straight stitch held by a few rows of horizontal straight stitch at intervals.
- Try weave stitch (see chapter 3).
- Try a 'drunken wiggle' with loops incorporated, but make sure it is interlocked by making the stitch wavy and using the loops.
- Try rows of open zigzag backwards and forwards and overlapping. (This needs to be worked heavily.)
- Try working with automatic stitches. Wave stitch and three-step zigzag can be interesting. Choose a wide stitch width and work slowly backwards and forwards, stitching rows side by side. The extreme width of each stitch pattern should interlock with the extreme widths of the adjoining row to produce a net. This is a difficult stitch to master, but very effective when done.
- Try creating a fairly tightly worked grid of straight stitching and adding automatic stitch patterns to it.

Vanishing fabric lace with pieces of copper added. (Worked by Lynn Revill, a graduate of Manchester Polytechnic.)

- Machine with a fine whip stitch or corded whip stitch. Ensure that the stitching is interlocking, or work on a previously made grid.
- Try cable stitch, as above. If all the embroidery is done with a cable stitch, either side of the work will be suitable as the right side. Cable stitch could be used as a 'gimp' on a lace design.
- Try adding small pieces of fabric and stitching over them.
- Waste threads can also be cut up and added.
- Look at traditional lace designs and try to copy some of the patterns used.
- Try applying ribbon to the design.
- Create a lace structure by stitching large overlapping circles over waste threads.

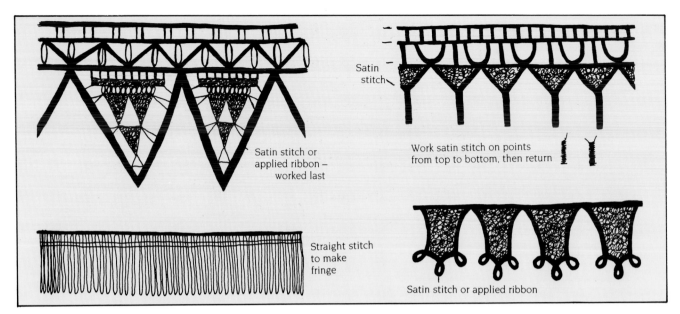

Satin stitch

Satin stitch or applied ribbon – worked last

Work satin stitch on points from top to bottom, then return

Straight stitch to make fringe

Satin stitch or applied ribbon

Project 17

- Design and work a formalized piece based on an open lace structure and using satin stitch as a strengthening 'gimp'. Remember that satin stitch will only work over rows of straight stitching.
- Designs based on the above technique could be derived from plant forms, leaf structures (look at the lace structure of decaying leaves), shells, windows, buildings, rock formations, and so on.
- Create an all-over lace design – try small overlapping circles, where the design (perhaps pictorial) is incorporated through colour change.
- Try a metallic thread on the bobbin and coloured thread on top.
- Add small pieces of fabric in an organized way to build up colour concentrations or a geometric design.
- Try to overcome the temptation to overstitch and make heavy lace structures – experiment to see how fine a lace structure can be yet still hold together in a useful piece. A more open structure will be possible if a small amount of stiffening residue is left in the fabric after vanishing.
- Try a large piece of work based on a garden, building, cityscape or magnified natural image. The design source should offer the possibility of different lace structures. Try to create a piece that will hang independently when it is finished.
- Create laces suitable for border and edge motifs for garments, interiors or pictures and hangings.
- Try making fringes by working straight stitch rows onto a structure or attached to a fabric.

Edges taken from traditional needlelace designs could be worked on vanishing fabric.

If lace structures are carefully designed and made they should be capable of hanging freely and independently, and of being used for any purpose. They can be washed and worn if handled with due care. The more robust the structure, the better will be its handling qualities. So, if a piece of work will have to withstand wearing, and is not attached to any fabric whatsoever, it is best to create it out of an interlacing grid or overlapping circles and then add the design. Less rigid structures will work well on collars, pictures, hangings, or for lace curtains or edges.

Worksheet of window designs which could be used as a starting point for vanishing fabric work. The central window comes from Mackintosh's Willow Tea Rooms in Glasgow. The large window on the right is from the Hoover factory on the Western Avenue, London.

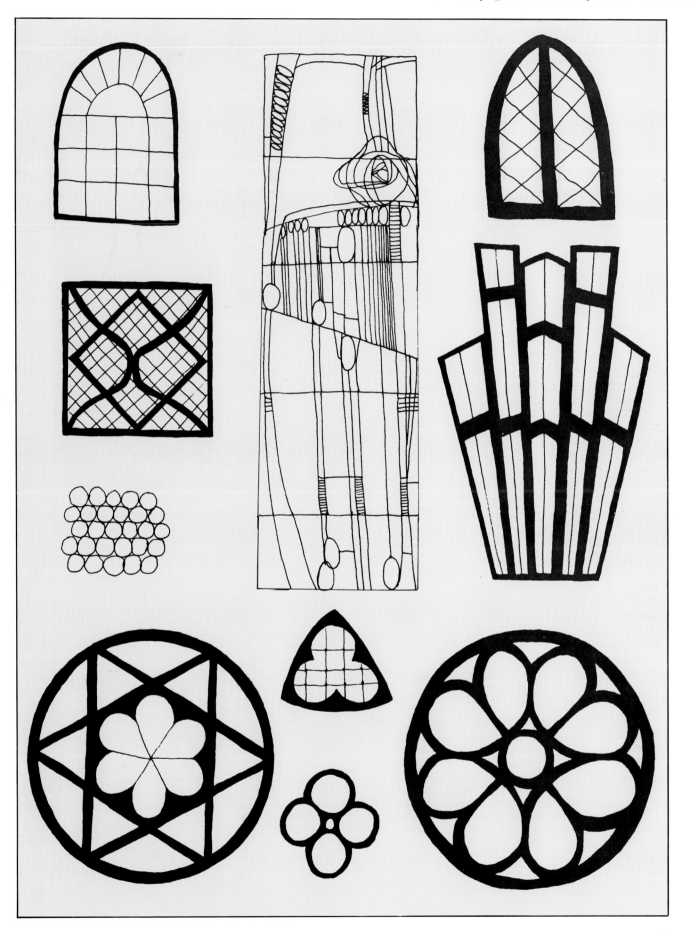

Reclining figure Scrim worked over in pulled work with a metallic thread (see chapter 7), placed onto a silk noile ground and stitched further. The figure is applied layers of transparent fabric, cool and warm colours used to indicate shadow and light. The border is worked on hot water vanishing fabric.

Lace fabric made on vanishing muslin with pieces of fabric added. A commercial multi-needled schiffli machine was used to lay the embroidered groundwork of this particular fabric for the sake of speed as a repeat motif was used. Embroidery was then added using a domestic machine. (Worked by Nigel Cheney whilst a student at Manchester Polytechnic.)

Creating lace structures for appliqué

Care and attention is necessary when creating lace structures which are to be applied or bonded to other surfaces as the lace will still have to hold together when the fabric is vanished. However, the need for it to hold its shape on its own will be obviated as it is to be attached to another piece of fabric, and also any repairs will be easier, so the design can be a little less strict: leaves, flowers on stems, unattached branches or trees, very openly worked windows or gates, or simply textural pieces. These can be worked on vanishing fabric and then bonded; lightly stab stitched to the surface of an embroidery; or attached by further machine embroidery stitching for added texture – but be careful that the lace is not flattened by too much extra stitchery.

Such work, created independently and then added to embroideries, can be very impressive, adding depth, texture and a three-dimensional effect. But bear in mind that any stitching worked on the vanishing fabric will count for double when the fabric is dissolved as both the bobbin thread and top thread will be visible and add to the bulk when applied to the fabric surface. The residue sometimes left in water vanishing fabrics can be useful for moulding pieces of lace before the work dries; alternatively, wires can be incorporated to create very three-dimensional effects – a technique covered in chapter 7.

Project 18

- Try working leaves, flowers, grasses, windows or other structures, and applying them to an embroidery.
- The following technique can help when you are not sure where to put something, or what colour it should be: make the proposed object in vanishing fabric and move it around on the picture or change the colour before deciding where to attach it. (Of course a worksheet should already have sorted out such problems!)
- Try stitching some of a pattern onto the surface of a fabric, and working some of it onto vanishing fabric. The applied lace area will add a textural contrast.
- Try creating a whole foreground segment of an image on vanishing fabric to add depth to the picture – this could be a gate or archway to look through, or perhaps an overhanging tree.
- Try a design that starts as machine-embroidered fabric, continues with lace added, and finally becomes a structure of lace only.

Lace, worked on vanishing fabrics, can offer a beautiful fabric on its own, or it can add texture and interest to a piece of embroidery, but the design and structure need to be carefully planned and executed if the result is to be satisfactory. Experimenting with this relatively new technique will offer original innovations to your own embroidery, so any work will be repaid. But this is a slow technique; because the whole of the work is formed through the use of stitched threads (unless waste threads or fabric pieces are added) obviously a lot of stitching is involved. Quick haphazard stitching can offer interesting textures which can form a background for a piece of embroidery but neater and more careful work will be rewarding if a piece is really to stand out and be true to its conception.

Samples of lace attached to a surface using water as a source of inspiration. Top left Fish worked in straight and satin stitch, with open and closed areas of stitching, applied to a turquoise silk ground. Top right Offcuts of threads and bits of fabric stitched with metallics onto cold water vanishing fabric. This is then applied to a ground and further stitched. Bottom left Zigzag in a variegated thread where some rows are deliberately allowed not to catch their neighbours. As the work was drying it was over-stretched so that these gaps would become holes. The lace was stitched down with metallic threads in a circular motion to increase the effect of these 'bubbles'. Bottom right This sample is made up of two pieces of vanishing lace; the fine net on the surface would not hold its shape if it were not stitched to a surface. The lace underneath is worked with an overlapping vermicelli stitch from an automatic stitch on the Pfaff Creative 1473 machine.

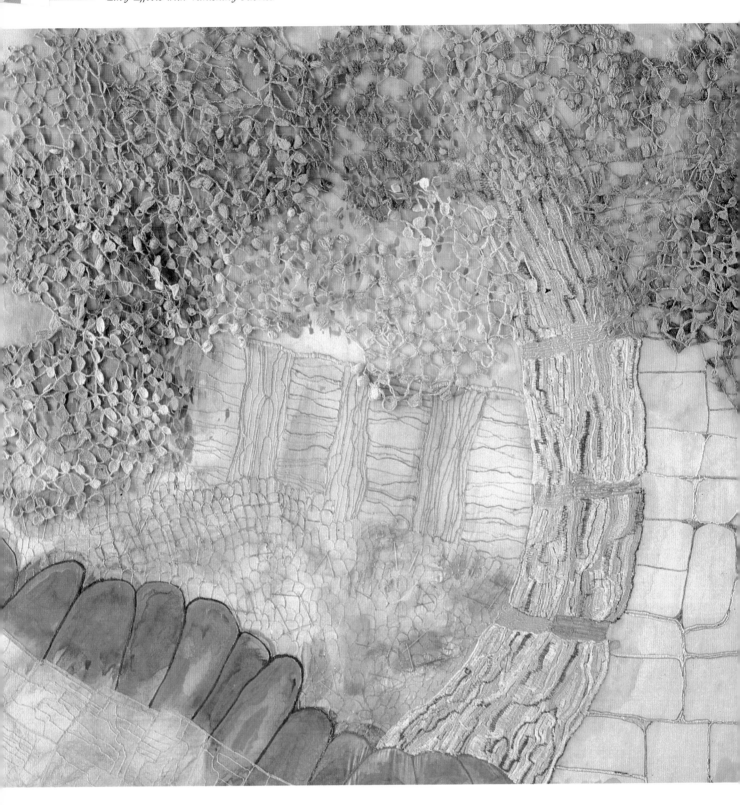

Buttermarket, Chipping Campden *Worked on a dyed habutai silk ground. The leaves, through which the scene is viewed, are worked on hot water vanishing fabric and stitched on. Pieces of chiffon are added by hand to give the texture of the slabbed area. (Worked on an Elna machine by Roma Edge.)*

7
Textural Techniques and Unusual Surfaces

Machine embroidery on its own can offer many textural possibilities. The choice of stitch design and tension, making holes in fabric or incorporating vanishing fabric laces can add much to a design. But as well as working on more 'normal' fabrics (does it *always* have to be calico?), other surfaces can offer much interest to machine embroidery, either as a surface for embroidery or as interesting textures to apply to other areas of embroidery. In this chapter I aim to look at a few of my favourites and some of the most popular, and discuss how these can be used.

Nets

The most widely available coloured nets are machine-made hexagonal-based nylon. The variety of colours available is virtually endless, and these fabrics are incredibly inexpensive. They are almost impossible to dye in the home, so choose the colours required – layering the nets together can give the impression of further colours.

A variety of netted fabrics are also available in nylon and natural fibres specifically for curtaining, the natural fibres being easier to dye than nylon. In specialist shops metallic nets can be bought, which are usually intended for evening wear or theatre costume. These are most often available in gold, silver and multicolours and can be found in diamond-shaped and square nets, and even large hexagons reminiscent of chicken wire, as well as small hexagonal nets with metallic threads woven in.

In order to machine on the looser nets it is necessary to put the fabric in a hoop and work with small stitches across the holes to create a lace network which will firm up the structure.

The firmer hexagonal nets can be stitched freely with the fabric in a hoop, or stitched with the foot on and the feed operating. They are particularly effective when used for free machine embroidery as the result is a little haphazard due to the structure of the net which makes a very exact design difficult, if not impossible. For nylon nets use a ballpoint needle. Remember also that the bobbin thread will be as important as the top thread as it will show a little on the finished piece of work. A greater amount of colour can be introduced through using a different bobbin colour, and tension techniques can also be used to increase texture.

Nets are obviously completely different from ordinary fabrics in their response to stitching; this will give

inspiration as to stitch and texture design. Stitched or unstitched, they can also be cut up and applied to a surface, with the advantage that most nets do not fray. Layers of different coloured nets can build up a richly coloured and textured surface. Stitching can be included for added texture or detail; again use a ballpoint needle. The nets can be held down before machining with pins, small tacking stitches, small pieces of bonding fabric, very small amounts of PVA glue, or use a darning foot or cocktail stick to hold loose pieces of net in place.

Transparent fabrics

A wide choice of transparent fabric is now available: silk and nylon chiffons, cotton organza, silk organdie, and polyester shimmer fabrics – some of which are 'shot' (the warp and weft are of different colours). These fabrics are generally available at good fabric shops, or theatrical or Asian fabric shops. They can be stitched on, perhaps delicately, to create a beautiful fabric in their own right; layered together and then areas cut out to create shadow or 'mola' work; or small pieces can be cut out and applied to a background fabric.

Chiffons and organdies can be stretched by pulling with your fingers or stitched along edges on the cross, thereby creating interesting curls and structures. Synthetic fabrics can be treated by burning to create a more interesting surface which can then receive further stitching, or the burning can be used to create edges and holes through which one might glimpse an intriguing background. The burning needs to be carefully controlled, so use an old soldering iron or a joss stick.

The same rules apply as for net: use a ballpoint needle for all these fabrics, the finer the better; consider the importance of the bobbin thread to the design; and any pieces applied to a surface can be done in the same way.

These fabrics also work well when incorporated into vanishing fabric lace as their delicate quality complements the finely stitched lace structure and they also provide increased insurance against the lace falling apart – this may be important to the novice!

Metallic fabrics

Metallic fabrics are available at good fabric stores where they are likely to be in demand for evening wear –

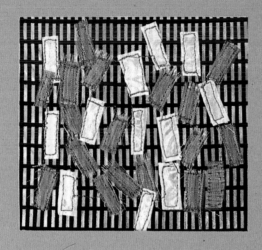

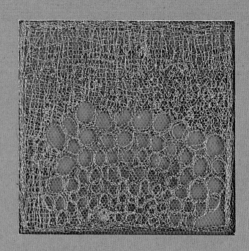

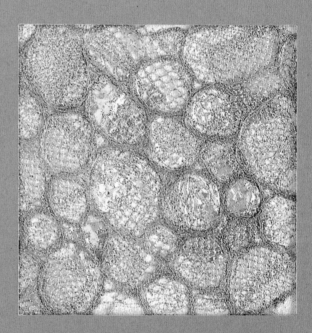

Christmas is the best time to find them – or try theatrical fabric shops.

Again the choice is wide, from heavily knitted fabrics to finely woven tissue. Some of these fabrics are fray-resistant, others, particularly the tissues, fray badly. It is also necessary to be cautious when ironing – do a test first. Fraying can be mitigated by applying bonding fabric, or using an iron-on backing. If these precautions are not

Samples from Project 19. Top left Mother of pearl fabric applied to a metallic fabric. Bottom left Transparent fabrics cut up and placed onto a background with free machine embroidery worked in metallic threads to hold the pieces in place. The inspiration for this piece was 'The Kiss' by Gustav Klimt. Top right Weave stitch and circles worked in a variegated metallic thread on net. Bottom right Layers of gold net in different densities, gold tissue, and gold circles worked on vanishing muslin laid down with further stitching. The inspiration for this piece was the shower of gold for the Danae picture, for which this was a sample.

suitable the fabric can be applied to a surface and the edges stitched over with free machine embroidery or a slightly open satin stitch, or use a reverse appliqué method (see chapter 5).

A ballpoint needle is essential for all metallic fabrics.

These fabrics can be a little overpowering on a large scale, so they are probably best used in small or medium-sized pieces applied in with other work, or apply a large piece but work over areas of it. Metallic fabrics can also be included in vanishing fabric work, but use cold water vanishing fabric to avoid using heat on these delicate materials.

Machine settings

As appropriate for the technique to be used.
Tension: Not over-tight. If using whip or feather stitch loosen the bobbin tension and only slightly tighten the top tension.
Needle: Fine ballpoint, 70–80. Use a larger needle if using a coarse metallic thread.

Project 19

- Experiment to create your own lace and net structures on as wide a variety of nets as possible. Embroidered lace on nets was first worked by machine in the 1870s – look at historical pieces for inspiration as well as personal experimentation.
- Try layering and cutting through nets, metallic fabrics and transparent fabrics. Consider suitable design sources: water, stained glass, layers of misty fields, fish, trees, flowers, and so on. Collect sketchbook work or photographs and magazine cuttings.
- Try piecing these fabrics onto a surface – use bonding fabric to hold them in place, and add stitching or layers of vanishing lace. Beads and hand stitches could be included, but keep any hand stitching simple.
- Create an intricately textured background which could then be used for an embroidery of a different nature, i.e. cutwork, stumpwork or fabric manipulation – cording, pintucking or smocking.

Paper

All paper can be stitched on, but some types will stand up to the treatment better than others. Essentially the stitching is creating perforations in the paper, so the closer the perforations, the more likelihood there will be of the paper tearing. The more malleable the paper, the less likely it is to tear; thicker papers and handmade papers, particularly cloth-based ones, are particularly resilient. Using larger stitches decreases the amount of perforations and so helps mitigate the problem – even the crispest paper can be stitched onto if a foot and feed is used with large straight stitches. Avoid satin stitch, instead use an open zigzag. When using a foot and feed, a 'teflon' or roller foot may be preferable to avoid marking the paper.

Papers, being stiffer than fabric, are easily stitched without a feed, out of a hoop and with no foot (although use a darning foot if you prefer). The paper should be held down firmly onto the bed of the machine with all the fingers.

More intense stitching can be worked onto a paper surface if it is first applied to a fabric, but choose a fabric of a suitable weight – something too heavy will spoil the delicate quality that can be achieved by stitching on paper.

The perforations can be used to good effect for a decorative pattern if the thread is removed. If the paper is closely stitched to a fabric surface excess paper to the design can be torn away, leaving paper appliqué in selected areas.

Handmade papers, tissues, wrapping papers and foils, thin card, ingres ... the list is endless, but the stiffer the paper the more it will wear the needle. Use a fine, sharp needle, but be prepared to throw it away after use or keep one especially for paper.

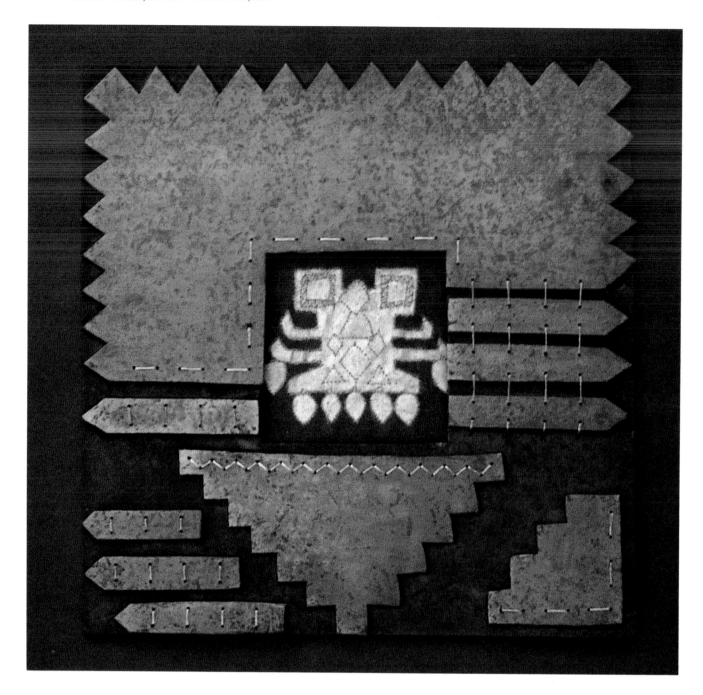

Leather and plastic

Leather and plastic can add texture if applied to an embroidery or they may be stitched on to create a fabric in their own right. Acetates and firm plastics have a lot to offer for embroidered sculpture, particularly mobiles and hangings. Leather can obviously be used for garment and accessory construction but gold, silver and coloured kids have a traditional place in metal thread work, and the machine can be exploited for this.

All such fabrics mark easily when using a feed and foot, so a 'teflon' or roller foot should be used. There are also needles with a special point for leathers and plastics which pierce the surface more cleanly – use as fine a needle as possible, particularly for plastics. Stitch carefully to avoid

Top **Fragments of El Dorado** *Tile made from stitched layers of raku-fired fine clay. The centre is worked by colouring a soft Japanese handmade paper with metallic oil pastels. This is then placed onto a silk ground and machined with small stitches with a darning foot. The unwanted paper is torn away leaving a soft edge.*

stretching the fabric, but stitches should be as large as possible to avoid too many perforations.

Free machine embroidery can be worked onto leather and plastic surfaces – it is better not to use a hoop, but experiment to see whether you prefer to use a darning foot. In order to maintain the integrity of the fabric it is necessary not to over-stitch; however, excessive amounts of stitching may destroy part of the fabric and thus add to the variety of texture in the finished work.

The range of uses for plastic as an embroidery material is as wide as the imagination: large kite-like structures for interiors, small, intimate pieces – a transparent pocket perhaps, carrying a special memento – boxes or patchworks, or modern jewellery pieces.

Leather has a history and tradition in embroidery that is more difficult to break free of, but dyed kids offer a new colour and textural dimension to appliqué which could be mixed with metallic fabrics and nets. Accessories need not be the obvious belts and bags but hats and other headpieces, or jewellery – earrings, necklaces and bangles for example.

Bottom **Fragments of El Dorado**. *Worked on black silk with metallic leather kids and forward and reverse straight stitching. The kids are also applied to the tile surface which is then layered, stitched and lustred.*

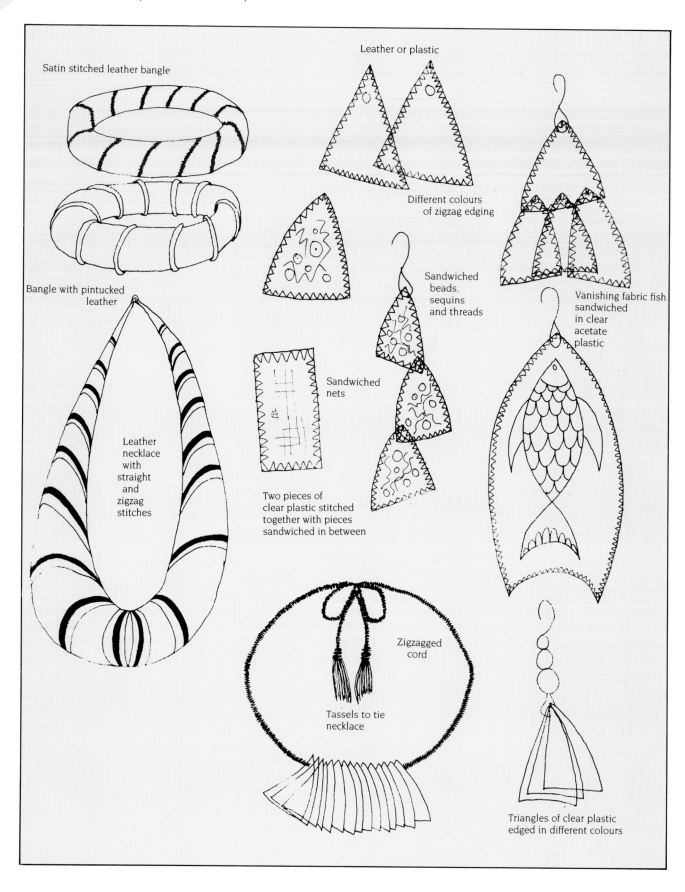

Satin stitched leather bangle

Leather or plastic

Different colours of zigzag edging

Bangle with pintucked leather

Sandwiched beads, sequins and threads

Vanishing fabric fish sandwiched in clear acetate plastic

Leather necklace with straight and zigzag stitches

Sandwiched nets

Two pieces of clear plastic stitched together with pieces sandwiched in between

Zigzagged cord

Tassels to tie necklace

Triangles of clear plastic edged in different colours

Worksheet of ideas for machine embroidery with knitting.

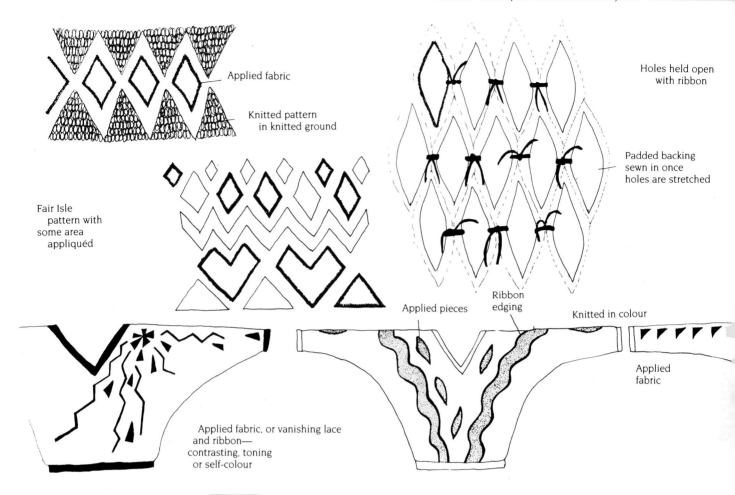

Worksheet labels (clockwise):
- Applied fabric
- Knitted pattern in knitted ground
- Holes held open with ribbon
- Padded backing sewn in once holes are stretched
- Knitted in colour
- Applied fabric
- Ribbon edging
- Applied pieces
- Applied fabric, or vanishing lace and ribbon— contrasting, toning or self-colour
- Fair Isle pattern with some area appliquéd

Knitted fabrics

Worksheet of ideas for machine embroidery with knitting.

Knitted fabrics, whether commercially made or home machine or hand knitted, have stretchability as an inherent quality. According to the work that you have in mind this can either be a help or hindrance.

The stretchy quality of knits can be exploited by pulling the fabric as it is sewn. Thus edges can be straight stitched (choose a double or treble stitch if the machine has one) and satin stitched, but whilst pulling the fabric in the direction of the work. As with edges on any work, the knitting can be cut after the rows of straight stitching before being oversewn with the satin stitch. The fact that the edge is pulled as the stitching is worked will give a crinkle finish to the edge. If you prefer a straight edge, use paper or stitch-and-tear along the edge to be sewn, as some pulling is inevitable.

If you appliqué onto knits you will also encounter the same problems of stretching. Back the work with stitch-and-tear, paper or a non-woven fabric such as 'Vylene' and work the embroidery or appliqué in the normal way. The excess paper or fabric can be removed after stitching.

Appliquéd flowers and leaves are a very obvious way of working onto knitted garments. A more imaginative way is to create something that is integral to the fabric. Patterns could be made to co-ordinate with knitted-in patterns. Slits could be made as a part of the knitted structure, or afterwards by machining and cutting. These could be

further stitched over and be threaded with ribbon or used as a base for reverse appliqué. Stitching or applied cords could be used as an all-over design on a knitted base.

The obvious use for such work is in exotic garments, but knits can also be used for pictures and hangings and interiors. As always, the best results will be obtained by not rushing into a piece of work, but through careful sampling and design worksheets.

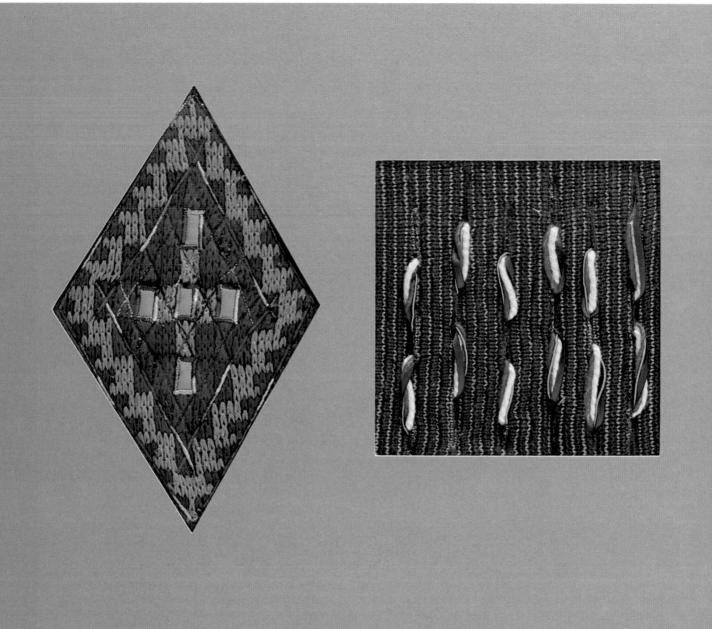

Samples of machine embroidery on knits. Left Satin stitched with foot on
and feed up (including appliqué); the straight stitch crosses are free
stitched. Right Automatic buttonholes made with a firm cross over stitch
and dual feed (Pfaff machine). These were laced with ribbon and cord.

Project 20

- Collect a variety of papers and try stitching on them with various machine patterns with the foot on and the feed up. Try making your own greetings cards or gift tags by applying paper foils to card.
- Try working on the various papers with free machine embroidery.
- Back the papers with a lightweight fabric and work on them.
- Try using papers as an integral part of an appliqué design, with cutwork or openwork, creating lace structures in areas cut out in firm papers, or dyeing or colouring the papers and using them as a surface in reverse appliqué.
- Work over and over on a paper until only the stitching is holding it together – experiment with texture in this way.
- Experiment with leather and plastic in appliqué. Try different methods of applying straight stitch, satin stitch, zigzag, or free machine embroidery over the edges to make the applied fabric integral with the base fabric.

Samples based on paintings by Gustav Klimt. Scrim, paper, painted plastic (with stained glass dyes) and pelmet 'Vylene' are all used to add texture to these pieces. (Worked by Barbara Vidal.)

- Try using leather and plastic with padded appliqué.
- Work into areas of hand or machine gold work.
- Create independent units of stitched and manipulated leather and plastic – pleated, tucked, pouches, boxes, 'kites' – and use them for mobiles, sculptures or jewellery. They could also be 'mixed with vanishing fabric lace.
- Try simple appliqué onto knitted surfaces with some machine stitchery.
- Try edges and cutwork on knitted surfaces.
- Try creating integral knitted and embroidered surfaces. Use 'Fair Isle' type pattern knitting, or 'Aran' type knitting manipulation as a base for the embroidery.

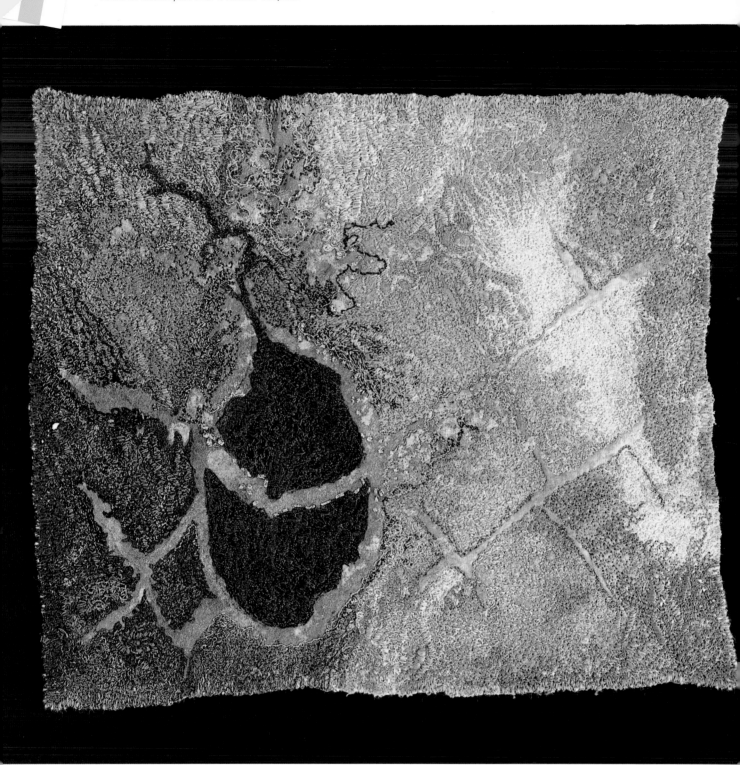

Felt

Felt is made from wool matted together through the use of heat, dampness and friction. It can be made in the home or bought in a number of colours and thicknesses. Because of its firmness it can easily be stitched using free machine techniques with or without a hoop, and with or without a darning foot. Its softness means that the result of stitching is rather like quilting – stitched areas are flattened,

Worked on a dyed thick commercial felt, this piece relies on heavy machine embroidery, much of it done with two threads in the needle at one time, to create movement and relief. Some hand seeding stitches were added to complete the work. The piece was inspired by the pattern made by tyre tracks in mud. (Worked by Eileen Bissel on a Bernina.)

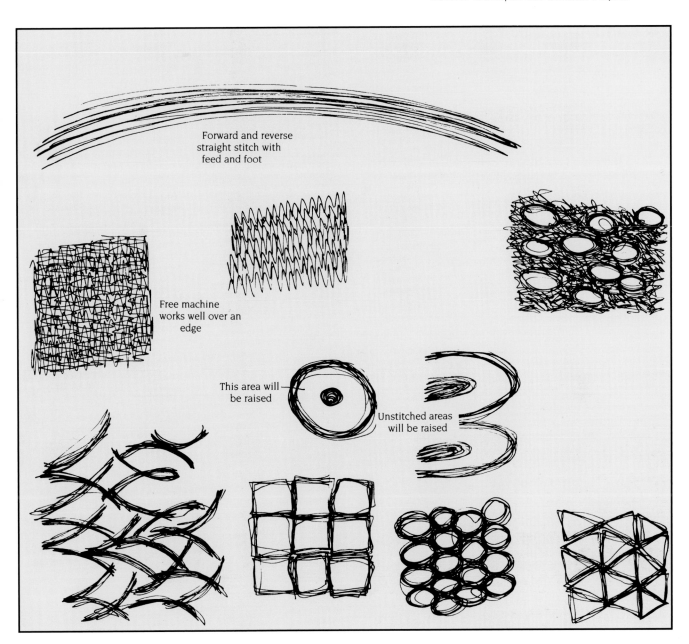

Forward and reverse
straight stitch with
feed and foot

Free machine
works well over an
edge

This area will
be raised

Unstitched areas
will be raised

unstitched areas are more raised. It is easily manipulated by the direction of stitching. Working in circles, curves, or heavy straight stitching over edges will all manipulate this pliable yet firm fabric into lumps, bumps and three-dimensional shapes. This process of manipulating a fabric surface can be achieved by stitching heavily onto almost any firm fabric, but felt reacts the most readily.

Any thread can be used, an ordinary needle and any tension techniques can be incorporated, but if fabric manipulation is the aim then tight tensions will be best, including a tightly tensioned cable stitch.

Felt has the advantage that it does not fray, so edges, holes and appliqué are easily worked.

If you are making your own felt you can experiment with the proportion of wool included in its composition, and include other offcuts of thread or fabrics (this can also be done with homemade paper). Dyed areas can be incorpo-

Stitches and pattern designs that could be used to manipulate felt. Note that tight tensions, cable stitching, using thicker threads or two threads at once will increase the effect.

rated, or wools can be dyed different colours before being made into the felt, and patterns or different textures of colour can be built up before the felting process starts.

Bought felt, being a natural fibre, is easily dyed. Silk dyes can be used as reactive ones are suitable for all animal fibres. Other dyes which are iron-fixable will also work, although iron fixing may flatten the surface a little.

Other fabrics can be stitched onto felt, or felt applied to other fabrics. Use an ordinary satin stitch, or work over all edges with a heavy build-up of free machine embroidery to make the fabrics more integrated.

Silk wadding and domette

These two fabrics, intended for use as quilt wadding, are available from specialist suppliers. They can be dyed, wetted, ironed, pulled and manipulated, and indeed used in the same way as felt.

Domette, being wool based, will give a similar matt quality to felt, but as it is based on a knitted surface the textures obtained will be different.

Silk wadding is a matted surface, like felt, but provides a much thicker fabric than any commercially available felt, even if it is treated by ironing in damp conditions. (This gives it a greater stability if the stitching is to be worked directly onto the wadding without a conventional fabric on either side.) The silk also has the benefit of a delicate surface sheen, rather than the matt finish or wool felt. If you are nervous about whether the silk wadding can take the amount of stitching planned in the design you can back it with a fine silk habutai before stitching. This stabilizes the structure further, without ruining its soft and flowing handling qualities.

It is best not to use a hoop on silk wadding as it will leave a mark, and anyway a tight drum-like surface will be practically impossible. The fabric is firm enough to be manipulated flat on the bed of the machine with a darning foot.

Domette, because of its knitted structure, can be worked in an embroidery hoop. Working on domette is like a cross between working on net, knitted fabrics and felt; the integrity of the structure must be maintained, may be enhanced, and the fabric can be flattened and manipulated as a felt.

Silk wadding will react like quilting on silk, or like a very thick felted wool. Stitching can be worked in fine quilting lines, or can be built up to flatten areas in the same way that felt can be manipulated. Excessive stitching, worked quickly and pulling at the fabric, can undermine its integrity – a quality that may be desired – or if excessive stitching is required whilst maintaining a more fabric-like quality, a backing fabric can be added as suggested.

Threads and fabrics can be loosely stitched on or carefully applied to these materials, or they themselves can be dyed and cut up and stitched onto other fabrics to add texture to a surface. As with felt, the best appliqué method is probably to work over the edges with free machine stitchery so that the fabrics become integrated through the stitching.

Machine settings

Set the machine appropriately for the technique required. For the most part these fabrics are best not used in a hoop, so set the machine feed down, use a darning foot, and your hands should be on the fabric on the flat bed of the machine.

Needle: Sharp, as fine as possible, 80–90 (thicker if using two threads).

Thread: Experiment with machine embroidery threads, and hand stitch threads for cable stitch, or use two threads at once – thread up as for a twin needle, or as for normal sewing, but put both threads through the eye of the needle.

Tension: As desired for the technique – tight if the felt surface is to be manipulated.

Project 21

- Experiment with stitching on felt – try to maintain a flat surface, and then see how much relief can be caused through stitching.
- Try cutting holes or slits in the felt and working over the edges – try free machine stitchery in different directions along the edges, or over the edges.
- Apply small pieces of thread and offcuts of fabric to the felt and incorporate neatly with satin stitch, or work heavily over the edges.
- Try applying felt to other fabrics. Dye the felt and surface fabric with similar colours, perhaps sponge-dyed, then add the felt and aim to integrate the fabrics through stitchery.
- Try all of the above techniques with silk wadding and domette.
- Work on silk wadding as if it were an ordinary quilted surface, including areas of light and heavily worked stitchery.
- Consider suitable design sources: architecture, patterns from ethnic sources, patterns in stonework or fences, tyre tracks in mud, plant drawings.

Samples of working with felts and waddings. Top *Worked on sponge-dyed silk, small pieces of dyed silk wadding are cut or torn and added to the surface, then the surface is stitched so that the wadding and silk become one. Gold thread is used throughout. The inspiration for this piece was the thermal springs on Rhodes, Greece.* Bottom *Worked on commercial felt, and using stitches with a tight tension on the top and in the bobbin, the felt is manipulated into small and large bumps. A holiday in North Africa inspired this piece.* (Bernina.)

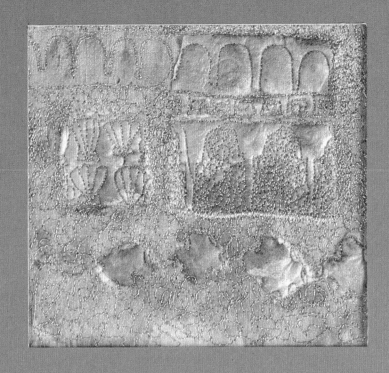

Canvas

Any type and size of embroidery canvas can be stitched on by hand and added to or applied onto other embroidery. A hand-stitched canvas could be left unfinished, applied to a firm background fabric, and then further enhanced with stitchery. If, however, the canvas is to support machine embroidery in its own right, then the size and type of canvas is very important.

To begin with, if the canvas is not an interlock or lockweave (different names for the same thing) then the effect of machine embroidery will be to create pulled work; this may be the desired end result, but it will make further even hand stitching practically impossible. If an interlock canvas is used the crossing over of the threads ensures that they do not move when they are stitched or pulled.

The choice of size of canvas, or number of threads to the centimetre, will make a difference to the sort of design that is possible. On page 14 there is an illustration of a rug canvas with the threads completely covered with a satin stitch – this would obviously be impossible on a fine canvas. However, if a finer canvas is used, then, as with canvaswork, an intricate design can be accomplished with machine embroidery. The closer together the threads are the easier and more accurate the stitching can be. If a satin stitch is to be worked then a finer canvas will also allow a wider choice of stitch widths as the satin stitch will be secured by how many threads it can be worked over (just as with a hand-stitched satin stitch). For this reason, if accuracy in a design is desired then the finer the chosen canvas the better, and seven threads to the centimetre (eighteen threads to the inch) is the best choice.

Working on a canvas of this type, hand stitchery can be included with machine embroidery. Hand stitches can be done and machine embroidery added, working around the existing stitches or encroaching into them; hand stitches can also be added to areas of machine embroidery if some holes are deliberately left open so that they will easily take stitches. This can be done quite haphazardly and the resulting hand stitchery will add an unexpected and informal texture, or it can add a kind of formality if traditional canvaswork stitches are used.

Appliqué is easily worked on canvas as the firmness of the canvas surface will hold a shape well while it is applied, but do this at the start of working before the canvas goes out of shape.

The needle should be of medium weight and sharp in order to penetrate the cotton threads of the canvas. The work does not need to be in a hoop, as the firmness of the canvas will make it possible to move and stitch on without one; however, it is wise to use a darning foot to prevent needle breakage.

Machined canvaswork has a tendency to go badly out of shape so it will need stretching afterwards – see Conclusion, page 113.

Project 22

- Experiment with stitches by hand and machine on a variety of canvases, including normal weave as well as interlock. Try canvases with different gauges of threads to the inch or centimetre.
- Working on seven threads to a centimetre (eighteen threads to an inch) or your preferred choice, experiment with appliqué, padded appliqué, stitching by machine over hand, hand over machine. Try copying hand stitches with the machine. Use automatic stitches.
- Explore design sources: architecture, flowers, fruit, vegetables and other typical canvaswork themes, ethnic patterns, Impressionist paintings (or your own); or paintings by any other artists you admire might form a starting point, for example Rousseau, the Cubists, Matisse, Hockney, Kandinsky.

Wisteria archway *Worked on interlock canvas using machine embroidery and some traditional canvaswork stitches. This piece was considerably out of shape when finished, but the final result shows the difference that stretching can make. (By Eileen Bissel.)*

Evenweave fabrics and scrim

Evenweave fabrics, even when made with cotton and synthetic fibres instead of linen, are expensive as a fabric for machine embroidery. However, it should be noted that machines can produce a 'hand embroidered' appearance of pulled work edges (using zigzag, four-sided stitch, or other automatic stitches and a tight tension), so if the desired object is a 'hand embroidered' linen tablecloth there really is no need to consign the next five years of your life towards not finishing it!

On a more creative note, scrims, usually in linen or cotton/linen union, and woven reasonably evenly, are inexpensive and very exciting. They can be purchased in dark ecru, white, and sometimes in colours. If the scrim feels stiff, it is best to wash it to remove some of the dressing, and it can of course be dyed.

Scrims can be worked on with the foot and feed in operation. If they are stiff a tight tension will be required in order to pull the theads together, but this is not so necessary on the soft coloured scrims. Automatic stitches can be used, or satin stitch can be carefully employed to achieve effects similar to hand-pulled work.

To use scrims with free machine embroidery you must place them in a hoop. Stitches based on satin stitch are the most successful as these work over a number of threads, pulling them together and distorting the structure of the fabric. It is this haphazard distortion which attracts me to this technique, as it can be used to add interest to a piece of work, or you can attempt to control the distortion.

In order to create a more textured surface on a piece of embroidery, scrims of different colours can be machined over with a fairly close zigzag of varying widths and in varying colours; these can then be applied to a surface and worked over again to increase the texture (see example of reverse appliqué in chapter 5 and the detailed illustrations of the wall hanging 'Danae being seduced by Zeus' on pages 1–3.)

For a completely different effect a coloured scrim can be used as the sole base fabric for an embroidery. If a straight or zigzag stitch is worked from side to side on the scrim the result will look a little like free pattern darning. If worked forwards and backwards a more haphazard result will emerge that can be stitched over and over. Using different colours, stitch widths, density of zigzag and satin stitch, different movements of the hoop – straight lines, circles, etc, and perhaps the occasional straight stitch – an impression of an image begins to emerge. Bits of thread or offcuts of fabric can also be included.

A sharp fine needle is used for this technique, although a heavy build-up of stitches may require a coarser needle in order to pass through comfortably. If subtle colour build-up is required, the finer the thread, the better. It is best not to use a darning foot unless the work becomes very thick, as a great deal of accuracy is needed if a fairly exact image is to be created. Large pieces can become misshapen, so stretch when finished and occasionally whilst working if accuracy and straight lines are required. (For notes on stretching, see Conclusion page 112.)

Project 23

- Try satin stitching and automatic patterns on soft scrim; vary the tension, including tight tensions, as well as trying whip and feather stitch.
- Work a heavy, close zigzagged background. The movement should be forwards and backwards in a wavy motion. This can then be applied to a surface and

Stitch designs for free machine embroidery and automatic stitch patterns suitable for working on scrim.

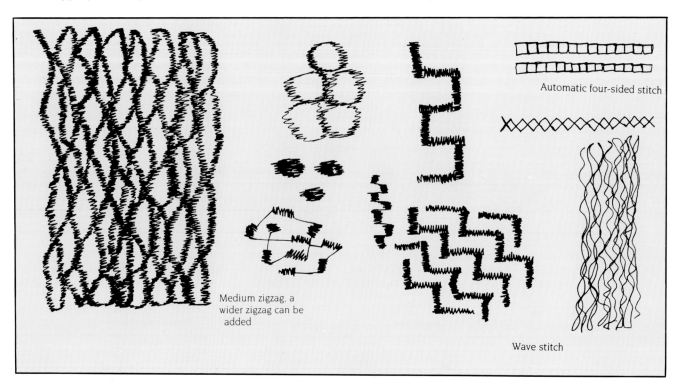

Medium zigzag, a wider zigzag can be added

Automatic four-sided stitch

Wave stitch

additional stitchery added — a good choice is 'weave stitch' as this works into and resembles the remaining threads of the scrim.

- Try working on scrim alone: try a pattern darning effect using a side-to-side motion.
- Work in any direction that seems necessary to create a desired image — garden subjects are a good starting point. It is easiest if the scrim has a base work of wavy zigzagged lines on it first so that it has some stability

Examples of various stitches worked on fine soft linen/cotton scrim in a variegated and metallic thread. Free machine embroidery and automatic stitches were used. (Bernina.)

before additional stitching is added. Try working with the movements and tension techniques suggested in chapters 3 and 4 and compare the results to see which techniques are most successful.

● Explore design sources: garden subjects (particularly herbaceous borders), architecture, water, paintings by yourself or others, pastels (soft or oil) are particularly good for design drawings for this soft-edged technique. Try woods, forests, landscapes – in fact, anything!

I have only scratched the surface of the sort of textures and fabric manipulation possibilities inherent to a variety of fabric and non-fabric surfaces. If you add all the techniques discussed in the preceding chapters, some imagination and a great deal of sampling you will see that the potential is limitless – there are so many things that could be attempted that becoming truly innovative is not only possible but irresistible.

Samples of machine embroidery on scrim. Top right Circles and spirals worked with tight tensions on a scrim with a metallic line woven through. Top left Zigzag stitching in many directions and colours creates this colourful piece on soft blue scrim, inspired by drawings from ethnic beads. (Worked by Eileen Bissel on a Bernina.) Bottom left Blue and green scrims were treated with wavy zigzag lines to create a textured pulled base; this was stitched down to a noile surface and further stitching was added. Inspired by and worked from a late summer garden. Bottom right Zigzag stitching worked horizontally onto a soft scrim base. The overhanging tree and water lilies are worked with a vertical zigzag.

Working in relief and three dimensions

Working embroidery that is more than simply a surface has been popular since the stumpwork of the seventeenth century, and machine embroidery lends itself to relief and three-dimensional techniques.

Machine embroidery will stiffen a fabric by virtue of heavy stitching alone, and if the direction of this stitching is also considered the fabric can be manipulated by the stitching to take on certain shapes.

Many of the techniques discussed in chapter 5 are useful for creating edges on pieces of work that are to be used in relief or three-dimensionally, and lace created on vanishing fabric can also be applied in relief or used to create objects that are completely free-standing.

Should these pieces need stiffening for the nature of the design, stitching, quilt wadding, bonding fabric between two layers of fabric, pelmet 'Vylene', starch, thinned PVA glue, and wire can all be used.

Wire can be sewn into seams, or satin stitched over onto the surface of the work to add rigidity to edges or veins of

Medieval fragments *Tiles made from fine raku-fired clay are joined with copper rings, and hung from a copper tube. The tiles have holes around the centre so that the embroidery can be attached with stitching.*

leaves, or anything else deemed appropriate. A medium-weight florist's wire, or similar, is best. If too fine a wire is used and the needle hits it, it can enter into the bobbin race area of the machine and may cause damage if stitching is not stopped immediately. If a thicker wire is used, it may be easier to see and so avoid hitting; if it is struck by the machine needle, the needle will probably break, but this is better than damaging the machine! All stitching should be done slowly as then the needle is more likely to slide off the wire and not break. Wire can also be stitched onto a finished (though not vanished) vanishing fabric lace in areas where a 'gimp' thread might be used. A fine satin stitch will secure the wire. The resulting lace

Medieval fragments, *a close-up. The lustres on the surface of the tile have been 'reduced' and the tile surface smoked by the process of raku firing, where a tile is removed from the kiln in a red hot state and immersed in sawdust, and finally in water. The embroidered square is metallic threads on a cold water vanishing fabric base. The diamond layer is worked on a pink soft scrim. First a grid of variegated metallic satin stitch was worked with the foot on and feed up, then various colours were added with a straight stitch and free machine embroidery into the squares in the grid. The embroidery is attached with a hand running stitch through the holes in the surface of the tile.*

structure will be very much like the wired needle-made lace used for stumpwork – with the advantage that it is much quicker! Wire can also be wrapped on its own or with cords to be used for stems, branches and so on.

Abstract or abstracted designs may appeal, but the most popular area for this type of work has always been naturalism. Creating relief work or totally three-dimensional pieces based on natural subjects is fairly simple, usually successful, and will generally cause delight and amusement in an audience.

To design such pieces is straightforward. Simply take the object, whatever you have in mind – from a rose to a cabbage, a shellfish to a slice of pizza or gâteau – and study it thoroughly. Draw petal or leaf designs to show how dyeing or stitching could be done, and look carefully at the construction of the object, and the shapes and relative sizes of its constituent parts. Take photographs and/or do a number of pencil drawings until you fully understand the construction of the object you intend to make. Now you are the world's greatest expert on the construction of roses, cabbages or whatever, you will know how to make the component parts; what texture they should be – dyed, stitched or vanishing lace; how many pieces are required; what size to choose; and you will also know how to assemble them. It's simply a question of looking really hard at the source material.

House at Puéchabon *This close-up shows the top window.*

Window and balcony detail from
House at Puéchabon, Languedoc, France *Worked on scrim, the outlines for the main features were worked with a straight stitch onto a basic machined ground. The details were then worked in appropriate colours, mostly using a forward and backward movement with a zigzag stitch. Some areas, such as the pavement, are worked with the ring moving horizontally. The blue line around the edges of the paint colour on the house is worked with a satin stitch. The tiles and wrought iron balconies are done with a straight stitch. See completed embroidery on page 119.*

An embroidered garden by Roma Edge. The central embroidery is worked
by hand and has a padded frame. The hanging fuchsias were made by
putting two fabrics together and stitching a zigzag around the outside,
thereby creating three-dimensional shapes simply copied from nature, and
giving depth to a picture by providing a foreground interest.

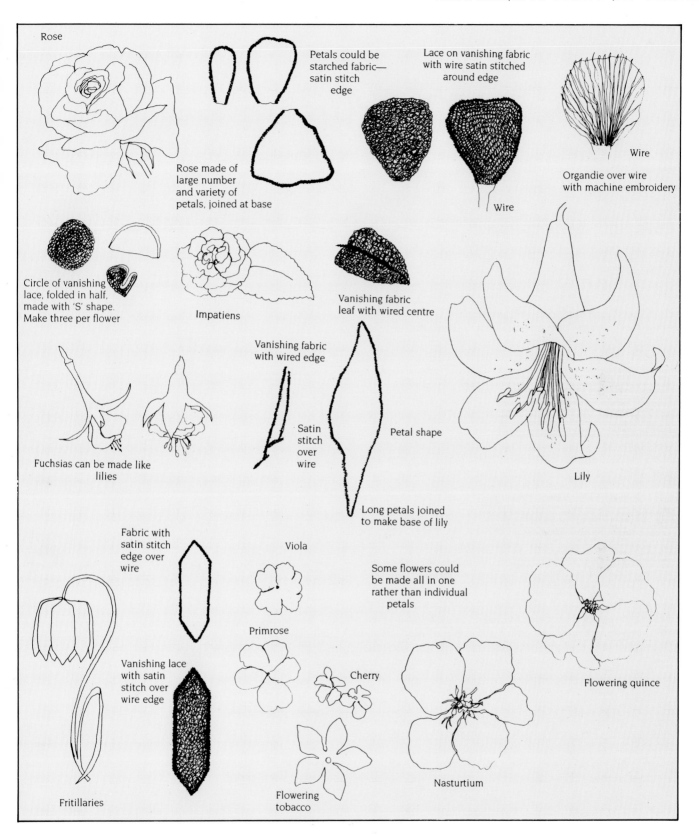

Rose

Petals could be
starched fabric—
satin stitch
edge

Lace on vanishing fabric
with wire satin stitched
around edge

Wire

Organdie over wire
with machine embroidery

Rose made of
large number
and variety of
petals, joined at base

Wire

Circle of vanishing
lace, folded in half,
made with 'S' shape.
Make three per flower

Impatiens

Vanishing fabric
leaf with wired centre

Vanishing fabric
with wired edge

Satin
stitch
over
wire

Petal shape

Lily

Fuchsias can be made like
lilies

Long petals joined
to make base of lily

Fabric with
satin stitch
edge over
wire

Viola

Some flowers could
be made all in one
rather than individual
petals

Flowering quince

Primrose

Vanishing lace
with satin
stitch over
wire edge

Cherry

Flowering
tobacco

Nasturtium

Fritillaries

Drawings of flowers with ideas of how they could be worked for
three-dimensional machine embroidery.

Conclusion

Collecting design ideas

It is a good idea to keep a small sketchbook and your favourite grade of pencil (and a pencil sharpener) with you at all times, then you can note down anything that may be of future interest to you. Working in a sketchbook every day, if only for ten minutes or half an hour, will improve your powers of drawing and observation, so that after a while the sketchbook will become a useful source and a matter of pride, instead of an embarrassment. Keep a folder or notebook for additional material – photographs, magazine cuttings, greetings cards, anything that appeals to you.

If a subject really interests you and you want to do a piece of work based on it, do not jump to an immediate conclusion about what technique to use, or what the image should look like – or indeed, what the finished piece should be. Collect as much visual information on the subject as possible: photographs, magazine cuttings, original drawings (preferably from the subject itself and not from the photographs). Put these together and look at them critically. Further drawing and sketching can also be done.

So many embroiderers treat this as some sort of penance before they can get involved in the exciting embroidery, but the value of collecting information and drawing copiously from it is that you begin truly to understand the subject, and, equally important, how you feel about it and wish to respond to it. Eventually an image might emerge, or ideas that could be tried for techniques.

Again, do not jump to conclusions about a particular technique, but start with one idea, and then see if you can rework it or add to it in some way. Don't accept too easily that something will *do* – be critical, can the idea or technique be improved on? After a good deal of sampling it may be necessary to refine the original idea or image. If not, the final piece can now be worked. Of course, with large embroideries, ideas are sometimes refined as the work progresses, but don't rush into any changes; think them through and, if necessary, prepare drawings and samples.

At the end of all this drawing and sampling you will find that you have enough material to create some attractive worksheets, or perhaps you have been working onto worksheets all along so that you could see how your ideas were progressing.

It may seem a lot of work for one piece of embroidery, but all the worksheets can be filed, and a portfolio of information – both technical and design – thereby built up for future reference, so next time you start a piece of work you already know what certain responses to certain images will look like, and these can thus be either eliminated or explored further.

Most importantly, although machine embroidery relies on 'craft' or technical expertise for its creation, it relies on 'art' or design for its aesthetic qualities if it is to be a success.

Finishing the work

It is important to realize that the work is not finished until it is properly presented.

There are many ways of making cushions, hangings, window mounts – card and fabric-covered – ideas on how picture framing should be done and so on, and there are books. However, before machine embroidery can be made up into the final object it will almost certainly need to be stretched. Any puckering or gross misshaping can usually be dealt with at this stage, and the final work, even if only a small sample for a presentation worksheet, will look that much better.

Embroidery, hand or machine stitched, is usually stretched by dampening the work, pinning it to a board, and leaving it to dry naturally. Once dry, any gums or starches in the fabric will help the final piece to maintain its shape. It is for this reason that natural fibres are the best ground to work on, although rayons, being cellulose based, are not too bad. With any other fabric problems may be encountered as the embroidery can regain its puckers when removed from the board.

Stretching embroidery

1 Use a plywood board about 1cm (½in) thick and cover it with a thin blanket or old flannelette sheet.
2 Dampen the embroidery by spraying with a garden spray – more water can be sprayed on during the stretching process if any wrinkles prove to be stubborn.
3 Place the embroidery face up on the board, and secure with drawing pins in the centre of each of the four sides, making sure the work is taut.
4 Now work outwards from those central pins, always pinning opposite sides, and stretching the work as you go, until the work is completely stretched and pucker-free.
5 Allow the work to dry naturally away from direct heat.

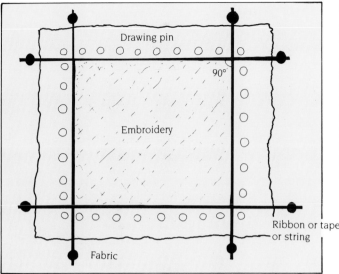

Plywood board

Drawing pin

90°

Embroidery

Ribbon or tape
or string

Fabric

The procedure for stretching embroidery where the squareness of the result is important.

Stretching large pieces to a given shape

If it is imperative that the sides be straight and square, and the embroidery started out that way, it is possible to return it to shape. Steps 1 and 2 remain the same.

3 Place the embroidery on the board, face up. Using a thick, easily visible thread, drawing pin lengths of thread to represent the four finished sides of the embroidery. The pins holding the thread should not go through the embroidered fabric, so each side will be represented by a long piece of thread, held by two pins (crossed in the appropriate places by two threads representing the sides running at right angles).

4 Start at a corner and pin one side to line up to the string. Adjoining sides can then be started. With this method, in order for the work to come to the right shape and hopefully the right size, it is necessary to respond to the problems as they arise. So, although adjoining sides should be worked in order, it is sometimes necessary to work opposite sides or finish off a corner; stretch one side a little, and then go back to it and stretch it some more; and so on until the embroidery is totally flat and the desired shape. Re-dampen as often as necessary.

5 Strong drawing pins will be required for a large piece. If these pull out of the work, use 1.5–2cm (¾in) carpet tacks. Note that no pins should be placed too close to the work as they may rust and cause stains.

Embroidered garment pieces can be stretched similarly – allow a large seam allowance for the drawing pins.

Dyed embroideries

If the fabric base for the embroidery is dyed or painted, and the colour fastness is doubtful, dampen the blanket and not the embroidery, to avoid any problems with the colours running.

Quilting or layered fabrics

Stretching quilted pieces can have the effect of flattening the work, so only stretch them if they really seem to need it. Any piece that is made up of layers of fabric, however, may need special treatment. If stretching all the layers together does not seem to remove all the puckers, then stretch each layer separately. Start with the bottom layer and pin it out as close to the embroidery as possible. Then stretch the next layer by pinning just outside this line; then the next and so on until all the layers are stretched. Just separating a piece into the topmost layers and bottom layer may be enough for most pieces.

Vanishing fabric lace

Water dissolvable laces may shrink a little or become misshapen, and this is particularly true of the hot water vanishing fabric. It is best to stretch these fabrics whilst they are still damp. Smaller pieces can often be pulled back into shape by hand. Laying the work out on a paper surface may help it to hold its shape. If the pieces are large then it is wise to have a record of what size they should be, and pin them back out to this size and shape. If the lace design and structure vary, it may be necessary to put pins in the work to hold certain areas; if so, dressmaking pins can be used, but it may be necessary to pin it out on a soft board or polystyrene. Allow the work to dry naturally, and do not iron as this increases stiffness.

Bear in mind that tighter lace structures shrink more and are more difficult to pull back into shape, but if this is done slowly and gently the lace fabric should not tear.

Canvaswork

Machine embroidery on canvas tends to cause the fabric to go out of shape even more than tightly worked canvas embroidery. Like canvaswork it needs to be stretched in a special way if it is to regain its shape and then hold it.

1 Use the board and string method as for large pieces of work (see above), so that the shape and size of the canvaswork can be predetermined. If the full size cannot be regained, the strings can be moved slightly as the stretching progresses.

2 Place the work upside-down on the board.

3 Starting at one corner and working along one edge, pin the work to the board so that it lines up with the string. It can be helpful if the work is slightly pulled longwise in the direction of the string.

4 Work an adjoining edge, and then the final two edges. It will seem as if there will never be enough fabric to come to shape, or alternatively, that there is far too much. Do not worry until the last pin is in. If the work is very out of shape it may be that drawing pins are not strong enough, so carpet tacks can be used.

5 If the work is very tight and cannot be pulled to shape it can be dampened as this will help. Also a piece of work can be dampened, stretched, pinned, and, if it is still not correct, dampened, stretched and pinned again, pulling a little harder. It is surprising how much give there is in a piece of canvas embroidery.

6 If the stretching has been done dry, the next stage can

follow immediately; if the work was dampened, wait until it is dry or the paste will penetrate to the front. Mix up some thick wallpaper paste and apply it, preferably with your fingers, to the exposed back of the canvas. If areas are lightly stitched or appliquéd avoid them, or apply the paste very thinly. The paste helps to ensure that the canvaswork will keep its shape.

7 Allow the work to dry naturally and remove it from the board. The embroidery may seem a little stiff. If it is to be used for a picture or hanging, this will not matter; if the canvaswork is for a cushion it will become softened in use quite quickly.

Stretching scrim embroideries

If the scrim has been added to other fabrics for extra texture, then the work can be treated as for normal or large embroideries. Small pieces worked solely on scrim may not even need stretching; if they do, treat them as normal embroideries.

Large scrim-only pieces need special care. When working a large piece, I map out the straight lines that I may require on the design, for example window frames, doorways, vertical plant structures, or any other important shapes such as ponds. Then I start work. If as the machining is added these lines no longer seem to be correct I then the work is stretched back into shape before any important areas are worked. Stretch the piece as for large embroideries back to an exact shape with verticals, horizontals and right angles. Then continue finishing off the work.

Stretching is repeated whenever it is deemed necessary, and of course at the end. Before the final stretching a piece of scrim embroidery can be a parallelogram rather than a rectangle, and very lumpy. After stretching it will be perfectly smooth but not always exactly the right shape – certain stitches pull the scrim more than others; large satin stitches, working from side to side with a large zigzag, or areas of zigzag worked in a circle, all pull the fabric in considerably more than just working up and down with a fine to medium zigzag. If this sort of stitching is required for the design it will be necessary to work a larger piece than you finally require – be careful about what is included towards the edge of the design as some of this may be lost.

And, finally . . .

Enjoy yourself! If you are used to the quiet relaxing atmosphere of hand embroidery, machine embroidery can seem over-fast, noisy and fraught. But, having learnt where the basic mistakes are to be made, and accepted that it is usually the operator's fault if the machine does not work correctly, it is usually possible to find the cause of any problems and deal with them yourself.

Remember to oil the machine regularly; look in the handbook for precise instructions for your machine; keep it dust-free by brushing out the bobbin race area after every sewing session and put a cover on it when it's not in use for periods of time. Electronic machines do not like extreme changes in temperature, so keep them in a suitable room. Always transport the machine upright – use a seatbelt if necessary! The machine should thus give you years of service, and after the initial fears and struggles you will find that it will become a true, reliable friend that will always bring something new to your work. You will also find that machine embroidery is at least as enthralling and engrossing as hand embroidery. Relaxing may be the wrong word to choose, but being alone with a machine, engrossed in making the machine do exactly what you want it to do, can certainly become a very real pleasure.

Gallery

House at Puéchabon – *see caption page* 109.

The Pond Worked by Karen Flemming who combines machine and hand embroidery techniques to create pieces, based on animals, that have the quality of relics.

Just Fish *by Frankie Creith.*

Pink Fish by Frankie Creith. The coastline of North Antrim, Northern Ireland provides the inspiration for these pieces. Various papers, paints, net, wadding and extensive free machine and hand stitching are used to build up work through many layers.

House at Giverny *by the author. Worked on fine linen scrim. Layers of machine embroidery colours are worked over the surface – some to create warm/cool juxtapositions, others are the 'real' colours. Zigzag, satin stitch, straight stitch and some set stitches are used to create the textured surface.*

Path in the Lake District *by Anne Booker. Worked by hand and machine on 18 threads to 1 inch interlock canvas.*

Samples on silk and hot water vanishing fabric lace for a Stuart style jerkin (17th century) by Lisa Collyer.

The Temptation Tapestry *Worked entirely by machine over scrim layered on to a silk noile surface (the scrim having firstly been worked over with metallic threads). Many techniques are used including tension techniques, satin stitch blocks (the ends are cut off), 9 mm satin stitch (Pfaff machine), and programmed stitches (Pfaff), the figures are 'bricked' straight stitch. In many areas two or three threads are used in the needle at one time. The piece is intended as a reworking of the Adam and Eve myth, where Eve is always to blame. In this image they are both culpable. The piece uses traditional Adam and Eve figures; the quality of the piece is intended to evoke Devonshire and tapestries.*

Bag worked on silk with vanishing fabric lace by Lisa Collyer.

Further Reading

Machine embroidery

Campbell-Harding, Valerie, and Watts, Pam, *Machine Embroidery: Stitch Techniques* (Batsford)

Hall, Carolyn, *The Sewing Machine Craft Book* (Van Nostrand Reinhold)

Hubbard, Liz, *Thread Painting* (David and Charles)

McNeill, Moira, *Machine Embroidery: lace and see-through techniques* (Batsford)

Risley, Christine, *Machine Embroidery – a complete guide* (Studio Vista)

Design

Holmes, Val, *Gardens in Embroidery Design* (Batsford)

Howard, Constance, *Embroidery and Colour* (Batsford)

Messent, Jan, *Embroidery and Architecture* (Batsford)

Helpful embroidery books

Butler, Ann, *The Batsford Encyclopedia of Embroidery Stitches* (Batsford)

Howard, Constance, *The Constance Howard Book of Stitches* (Batsford)

Lovesey, Nenia, *Creative Design in Needlepoint Lace* (Batsford)

Useful Addresses

Suppliers

Many of the following suppliers do mail order. Most will send a price list on receipt of a stamped, addressed envelope.

BARNYARNS,
Old Pitts Farm
Langrish
Petersfield
Hants GU32 1RQ

BOROVICKS
16 Berwick Street
London W1

Wide range of fabrics

CAMPDEN NEEDLECRAFT CENTRE
High Street
Chipping Campden
Gloucestershire

Superb range of machine threads;
also scrims and vanishing fabrics

CHOICES
36 Meadowside Road
Pangbourne
Reading
RG8 7NH

CREATIVE BEADCRAFT LTD
Unit 26
Chiltern Trading Estate
Holmer Green
High Wycombe
Bucks

NEEDLECRAFT NEEDS
11 Leigh Road
Wimbourne
Dorset BH21 1AB

SILKEN STRANDS
33 Linksway
Gatley
Cheadle
Cheshire SK8 4LA

SUE HARRIS
The Mill
Tregoyd Mill
Three Cocks
Brecon
Powys

Silk wadding

THREADBARE
Glenfield Park
Glenfield Road
Nelson
Lancs BB9 8AR

VOIRREY EMBROIDERY
Brimstage Hall
Brimstage
Wirral L62 6JA

WHALEYS (BRADFORD) LTD
Harris Court
Great Horton
Bradford
West Yorks

Water soluble fabrics (minimum order)

More suppliers can be found in *Embroidery*, a quarterly magazine published by the Embroiderers' Guild. Write to: Circulation Dept, PO Box 42B, East Molesey, Surrey KT8 9BB.

Embroiderers' Guild addresses

UK
THE EMBROIDERERS' GUILD
Apartment 41A
Hampton Court
East Molesey
Surrey KT6 9AU

USA
THE EMBROIDERERS' GUILD OF AMERICA
200 Fourth Avenue
Louiseville
Kentucky 40202

Australia
THE EMBROIDERERS' GUILD OF AUSTRALIA
175 Elizabeth Street
Sydney
New South Wales 2000

New Zealand
ASSOCIATION OF NEW ZEALAND EMBROIDERERS' GUILDS
171 The Ridgeway
Mornington
Wellington 2

Canada
CANADIAN EMBROIDERERS' GUILD
PO Box 541
Station B
London
Ontario N6A 4W1

Index